DEPARTMENT OF THE TREASURY
TECHNICAL EXPLANATION OF
THE CONVENTION BETWEEN
THE GOVERNMENT OF THE UNITED STATES OF AMERICA AND
THE GOVERNMENT OF ICELAND
FOR THE AVOIDANCE OF DOUBLE TAXATION AND
THE PREVENTION OF FISCAL EVASION
WITH RESPECT TO TAXES ON INCOME.

DEPARTMENT OF THE TREASURY
TECHNICAL EXPLANATION OF
THE CONVENTION BETWEEN
THE GOVERNMENT OF THE UNITED STATES OF AMERICA AND
THE GOVERNMENT OF ICELAND
FOR THE AVOIDANCE OF DOUBLE TAXATION AND
THE PREVENTION OF FISCAL EVASION
WITH RESPECT TO TAXES ON INCOME.

This is a technical explanation of the Convention between the Government of the United States and the Government of Iceland For the Avoidance Of Double Taxation and the Prevention of Fiscal Evasion with Respect to Taxes on Income, signed on October 23, 2007 (the "Convention").

Negotiations took into account the U.S. Treasury Department's current tax treaty policy, and the Treasury Department's Model Income Tax Convention. Negotiations also took into account the Model Tax Convention on Income and on Capital, published by the Organisation for Economic Cooperation and Development (the "OECD Model"), and recent tax treaties concluded by both countries.

The Technical Explanation is an official guide to the Convention and an accompanying Protocol. It reflects the policies behind particular Convention and Protocol provisions, as well as understandings reached during the negotiations with respect to the application and interpretation of the Convention and Protocol. References in the Technical Explanation to "he" or "his" should be read to mean "he or she" or "his and her."

ARTICLE 1 (GENERAL SCOPE)

Paragraph 1

Paragraph 1 of Article 1 provides that the Convention applies only to residents of the United States or Iceland except where the terms of the Convention provide otherwise. Under Article 4 (Resident) a person is generally treated as a resident of a Contracting State if that person is, under the laws of that State, liable to tax therein by reason of his domicile, citizenship, residence, or other similar criteria. However, if a person is considered a resident of both Contracting States, Article 4 provides rules for determining a State of residence (or no State of residence). This determination governs for all purposes of the Convention.

Certain provisions are applicable to persons who may not be residents of either Contracting State. For example, paragraph 1 of Article 23 (Non-Discrimination) applies to nationals of the Contracting States. Under Article 25 (Exchange of Information and Administrative Assistance), information may be exchanged with respect to residents of third states.

Paragraph 2

Paragraph 2 states the generally accepted relationship both between the Convention and domestic law and between the Convention and other agreements between the Contracting States. That is, no provision in the Convention may restrict any exclusion, exemption, deduction, credit or other benefit accorded by the tax laws of the Contracting States, or by any other agreement between the Contracting States. The relationship between the non-discrimination provisions of the Convention and other agreements is addressed not in paragraph 2 but in paragraph 3.

Under paragraph 2, for example, if a deduction would be allowed under the U.S. Internal Revenue Code (the "Code") in computing the U.S. taxable income of a resident of Iceland, the deduction also is allowed to that person in computing taxable income under the Convention. Paragraph 2 also means that the Convention may not increase the tax burden on a resident of a Contracting States beyond the burden determined under domestic law. Thus, a right to tax given by the Convention cannot be exercised unless that right also exists under internal law.

It follows that, under the principle of paragraph 2, a taxpayer's U.S. tax liability need not be determined under the Convention if the Code would produce a more favorable result. A taxpayer may not, however, choose among the provisions of the Code and the Convention in an inconsistent manner in order to minimize tax. Thus, a taxpayer may use the Convention to reduce its taxable income, but may not use both treaty and Code rules where doing so would thwart the intent of either set of rules. For example, assume that a resident of Iceland has three separate businesses in the United States. One is a profitable permanent establishment and the other two are trades or businesses that would earn taxable income under the Code but that do not meet the permanent establishment threshold tests of the Convention. One is profitable and the other incurs a loss. Under the Convention, the income of the permanent establishment is taxable in the United States, and both the profit and loss of the other two businesses are ignored. Under the Code, all three would be subject to tax, but the loss would offset the profits of the two profitable ventures. The taxpayer may not invoke the Convention to exclude the profits of the profitable trade or business and invoke the Code to claim the loss of the loss trade or business against the profit of the permanent establishment. (See Rev. Rul. 84-17, 1984-1 C.B. 308.) If, however, the taxpayer invokes the Code for the taxation of all three ventures, he would not be precluded from invoking the Convention with respect, for example, to any dividend income he may receive from the United States that is not effectively connected with any of his business activities in the United States.

Similarly, nothing in the Convention can be used to deny any benefit granted by any other agreement between the United States and Iceland. For example, if certain benefits are provided for military personnel or military contractors under a Status of Forces Agreement between the United States and Iceland, those benefits or protections will be available to residents of the Contracting States regardless of any provisions to the contrary (or silence) in the Convention.

Paragraph 3

Paragraph 3 specifically relates to non-discrimination obligations of the Contracting States under other agreements. The provisions of paragraph 3 are an exception to the rule provided in paragraph 2 of this Article under which the Convention shall not restrict in any manner any benefit now or hereafter accorded by any other agreement between the Contracting States.

Subparagraph 3(a) provides that, notwithstanding any other agreement to which the Contracting States may be parties, a dispute concerning whether a measure is within the scope of this Convention shall be considered only by the competent authorities of the Contracting States, and the procedures under this Convention exclusively shall apply to that dispute. Thus, procedures for dealing with disputes that may be incorporated into trade, investment, or other agreements between the Contracting States shall not apply for the purposes of determining the scope of the Convention.

Subparagraph 3(b) provides that, unless the competent authorities determine that a taxation measure is not within the scope of this Convention, the non-discrimination obligations of this Convention exclusively shall apply with respect to that measure, except for such national treatment or most-favored-nation ("MFN") obligations as may apply to trade in goods under the General Agreement on Tariffs and Trade ("GATT"). No national treatment or MFN obligation under any other agreement shall apply with respect to that measure. Thus, unless the competent authorities agree otherwise, any national treatment and MFN obligations undertaken by the Contracting States under agreements other than the Convention shall not apply to a taxation measure, with the exception of GATT as applicable to trade in goods.

Paragraph 4

Paragraph 4 contains the traditional saving clause found in all U.S. treaties. The Contracting States reserve their rights, except as provided in paragraph 5, to tax their residents and citizens as provided in their internal laws, notwithstanding any provisions of the Convention to the contrary. For example, if a resident of Iceland performs professional services in the United States and the income from the services is not attributable to a permanent establishment in the United States, Article 7 (Business Profits) would by its terms prevent the United States from taxing the income. If, however, the resident of Iceland is also a citizen of the United States, the saving clause permits the United States to include the remuneration in the worldwide income of the citizen and subject it to tax under the normal Code rules (*i.e.*, without regard to Code section 894(a)). However, subparagraph 5(a) of Article 1 preserves the benefits of special foreign tax credit rules applicable to the U.S. taxation of certain U.S. income of its citizens resident in Iceland. See paragraph 4 of Article 22 (Relief from Double Taxation).

For purposes of the saving clause, "residence" is determined under Article 4. Thus, an individual who is a resident of the United States under the Code (but not a U.S. citizen) but who is determined to be a resident of Iceland under the tie-breaker rules of Article 4 would be subject to U.S. tax only to the extent permitted by the Convention. The United States would not be permitted to apply its statutory rules to that person to the extent the rules are inconsistent with the Convention.

However, the person would be treated as a U.S. resident for U.S. tax purposes other than determining the individual's U.S. tax liability. For example, in determining under Code section 957 whether a foreign corporation is a controlled foreign corporation, shares in that corporation held by the individual would be considered to be held by a U.S. resident. As a result, other U.S. citizens or residents might be deemed to be United States shareholders of a controlled foreign corporation subject to current inclusion of Subpart F income recognized by the corporation. See, Treas. Reg. section 301.7701(b)-7(a)(3).

Under paragraph 4, the United States also reserves its right to tax former citizens and former long-term residents for a period of ten years following the loss of such status. Thus, paragraph 4 allows the United States to tax former U.S. citizens and former U.S. long-term residents in accordance with Section 877 of the Code. Section 877 generally applies to a former citizen or long-term resident of the United States who relinquishes citizenship or terminates long-term residency before June 17, 2008 if either of the following criteria exceed established thresholds: (a) the average annual net income tax of such individual for the period of 5 taxable years ending before the date of the loss of status, or (b) the net worth of such individual as of the date of the loss of status.

The United States defines "long-term resident" as an individual (other than a U.S. citizen) who is a lawful permanent resident of the United States in at least 8 of the prior 15 taxable years. An individual is not treated as a lawful permanent resident for any taxable year in which the individual is treated as a resident of Iceland under this Convention, or as a resident of any country other than the United States under the provisions of any other tax treaty of the United States, and in either case the individual does not waive the benefits of the relevant convention.

Paragraph 5

Paragraph 5 sets forth certain exceptions to the saving clause. The referenced provisions are intended to provide benefits to citizens and residents even if such benefits do not exist under internal law. Paragraph 5 thus preserves these benefits for citizens and residents of the Contracting States.

Subparagraph 5(a) lists certain provisions of the Convention that are applicable to all citizens and residents of a Contracting State, despite the general saving clause rule of paragraph 4:

(1) Paragraph 2 of Article 9 (Associated Enterprises) grants the right to a correlative adjustment with respect to income tax due on profits reallocated under Article 9.

(2) Paragraphs 2 and 4 of Article 17 (Pensions, Social Security, and Annuities) provide exemptions from source or residence State taxation for certain pension distributions and social security payments.

(3) Article 22 (Relief from Double Taxation) confirms to citizens and residents of one Contracting State the benefit of a credit for income taxes paid to the other or an exemption for income earned in the other State.

(4) Article 23 (Non-Discrimination) protects residents and nationals of one Contracting State against the adoption of certain discriminatory practices in the other Contracting State.

(5) Article 24 (Mutual Agreement Procedure) confers certain benefits on citizens and residents of the Contracting States in order to reach and implement solutions to disputes between the two Contracting States. For example, the competent authorities are permitted to use a definition of a term that differs from an internal law definition. The statute of limitations may be waived for refunds, so that the benefits of an agreement may be implemented.

Subparagraph 5(b) provides a different set of exceptions to the saving clause. The benefits referred to are all intended to be granted to temporary residents of a Contracting State (for example, in the case of the United States, holders of non-immigrant visas), but not to citizens or to persons who have acquired permanent residence in that State. If beneficiaries of these provisions travel from one of the Contracting States to the other, and remain in the other long enough to become residents under its internal law, but do not acquire permanent residence status (i.e., in the U.S. context, they do not become "green card" holders) and are not citizens of that State, the host State will continue to grant these benefits even if they conflict with the statutory rules. The benefits preserved by this paragraph are: (1) the host country exemptions for government service salaries and pensions under Article 18 (Government Service), certain income of visiting students and trainees under Article 19 (Students and Trainees), and the income of diplomatic agents and consular officers under Article 26 (Members of Diplomatic Missions and Consular Posts).

Paragraph 6

Paragraph 6 provides that an item of income derived by a fiscally transparent entity is considered to be derived by a resident of a Contracting State to the extent that the resident is treated under the taxation laws of the State where he is resident as deriving the item of income. This paragraph applies to any resident of a Contracting State who is entitled to income derived through an entity that is treated as fiscally transparent under the laws of either Contracting State. For example, if a corporation resident in Iceland distributes a dividend to an entity that is treated as fiscally transparent for U.S. tax purposes, the dividend will be considered derived by a resident of the United States only to the extent that the taxation laws of the United States treat one or more U.S. residents (whose status as U.S. residents is determined, for this purpose, under U.S. tax laws) as deriving the dividend income for U.S. tax purposes. In the case of a partnership, the persons who are, under U.S. tax laws, treated as partners of the entity would normally be the persons whom the U.S. tax laws would treat as deriving the dividend income through the partnership. Thus, it also follows that persons whom the United States treats as partners but who are not U.S. residents for U.S. tax purposes may not claim a benefit under the Convention for the dividend paid to the entity. Although these partners are treated as deriving the income for U.S. tax purposes, they are not residents of the United States for purposes of the treaty. If, however, they are treated as residents of a third country under the provisions of an income tax convention which that country has with Iceland, they may be entitled to claim a benefit under that convention. In contrast, if an entity is organized under U.S. laws and is classified as a corporation for U.S. tax purposes, dividends paid by a corporation resident in Iceland to the U.S. entity will be considered derived by a resident of the United States since the U.S. corporation is treated under U.S. taxation laws as a resident of the United States and as deriving the income.

Because the entity classification rules of the State of residence govern, the results in the examples discussed above would obtain even if the entity were viewed differently under the tax laws of Iceland (e.g., as not fiscally transparent in the first example above where the entity is treated as a partnership for U.S. tax purposes or as fiscally transparent in the second example where the entity is viewed as not fiscally transparent for U.S. tax purposes). Moreover, these results follow regardless of whether the entity is organized in the United States, Iceland, or in a third country. For example, income from sources in Iceland received by an entity organized under the laws of Iceland, which is treated for U.S. tax purposes as a corporation and is owned by a U.S. shareholder who is a U.S. resident for U.S. tax purposes, is not considered derived by the shareholder of that corporation even if, under the tax laws of Iceland, the entity is treated as fiscally transparent. These results also follow regardless of whether the entity is disregarded as a separate entity under the laws of one jurisdiction but not the other, such as a single owner entity that is viewed as a branch for U.S. tax purposes and as a corporation for tax purposes of in Iceland.

Where income is derived through an entity organized in a third state that has owners resident in one of the Contracting States, the characterization of the entity in that third state is irrelevant for purposes of determining whether the resident is entitled to treaty benefits with respect to income derived by the entity.

In general, paragraph 6 relates to entities that are not subject to tax at the entity level, as distinct from entities that are subject to tax, but with respect to which tax may be relieve under an integrated system. Entities falling under this description in the United States include partnerships, common investment trusts under section 584 and grantor trusts. This paragraph also applies to U.S. limited liability companies (("LLCs"), including an LLC with only one member), that are treated as partnerships or as disregarded entities for U.S. tax purposes. The taxation laws of a Contracting State may treat an item of income as income of a resident of that State even if the resident is not subject to tax on that particular item of income. For example, if a Contracting State has a participation exemption for certain foreign-source dividends and capital gains, such income or gains would be regarded as income or gain of a resident of that State who otherwise derived the income or gain, despite the fact that the resident could be exempt from tax in that State on the income or gain.

Paragraph 6 is not an exception to the saving clause of paragraph 4. Accordingly, paragraph 6 does not prevent a Contracting State from taxing an entity that is treated as a resident of that State under its own tax law. For example, if a U.S. LLC with members who are residents of Iceland elects to be taxed as a corporation for U.S. tax purposes, the United States will tax that LLC on its worldwide income on a net basis, without regard to whether Iceland views the LLC as fiscally transparent.

ARTICLE 2 (TAXES COVERED)

This Article specifies the U.S. taxes and the taxes of Iceland to which the Convention applies. With two exceptions, the taxes specified in Article 2 are the covered taxes for all purposes of the Convention. A broader coverage applies for purposes of Articles 23 (Non-Discrimination) and 25 (Exchange of Information and Administrative Assistance). Article 23 applies with respect to all taxes, including those imposed by state and local governments. Article 25 applies with respect to all taxes imposed at the national level.

Paragraph 1

Paragraph 1 identifies the category of taxes to which the Convention applies. Paragraph 1 is based on the U. S. and OECD Models and defines the scope of application of the Convention. The Convention applies to taxes on income, including gains, imposed on behalf of a Contracting State, irrespective of the manner in which they are levied. Except with respect to Article 23 state and local taxes are not covered by the Convention.

Paragraph 2

Paragraph 2 also is based on the U.S. and OECD Models and provides a definition of taxes on income, on capital and on capital gains. The Convention covers taxes on total income, on total capital, or any part of income and includes tax on gains derived from the alienation of property. The Convention does not apply, however, to social security charges, or any other charges where there is a direct connection between the levy and individual benefits. Social security and unemployment taxes (Code sections 1401, 3101, 3111 and 3301) are excluded from coverage. The Convention also does not apply to property taxes, except with respect to Article 23.

Paragraph 3

Paragraph 3 lists the taxes in force at the time of signature of the Convention to which the Convention applies.

The existing covered taxes of Iceland are identified in subparagraph 3(a). These taxes are i) the income taxes to the state and ii) the income taxes to the municipalities.

Subparagraph 3(b) provides that the existing U.S. taxes subject to the rules of the Convention are the Federal income taxes imposed by the Code, together with the excise taxes imposed with respect to private foundations (Code sections 4940 through 4948)..

Paragraph 4

Under paragraph 4, the Convention will apply to any taxes that are identical, or substantially similar, to those enumerated in paragraph 3, and which are imposed in addition to, or in place of, the existing taxes after October 23, 2007, the date of signature of the Convention. The paragraph also provides that the competent authorities of the Contracting States will notify each other of any significant changes that have been made in their laws, whether tax laws or non-tax laws, that affect significantly their obligations under the Convention. Non-tax laws that may affect a Contracting State's obligations under the Convention may include, for example, laws affecting bank secrecy.

ARTICLE 3 (GENERAL DEFINITIONS)

Article 3 provides general definitions and rules of interpretation applicable throughout the Convention. Certain other terms are defined in other articles of the Convention. For example, the term "resident of a Contracting State" is defined in Article 4 (Resident). The term "permanent establishment" is defined in Article 5 (Permanent Establishment). These definitions are used consistently throughout the Convention. Other terms, such as "dividends," "interest" and "royalties" are defined in specific articles for purposes only of those articles.

Paragraph 1

Paragraph 1 defines a number of basic terms used in the Convention. The introduction to paragraph 1 makes clear that these definitions apply for all purposes of the Convention, unless the context requires otherwise. This latter condition allows flexibility in the interpretation of the treaty in order to avoid results not intended by the treaty's negotiators.

The geographical scope of the Convention with respect Iceland is set out in subparagraph 1(a). It encompasses the territory of Iceland, including its territorial sea, and any area beyond the territorial sea within which Iceland, in accordance with international law, exercises jurisdiction or sovereign rights with respect to the sea bed, its subsoil and its adjacent waters, and their natural resources.

The geographical scope of the Convention with respect to the United States is set out in subparagraph 1(b). It encompasses the United States of America, including the states, the District of Columbia and the territorial sea of the United States. The term does not include Puerto Rico, the Virgin Islands, Guam or any other U.S. possession or territory. For certain purposes, the term "United States" includes the sea bed and subsoil of undersea areas adjacent to the territorial sea of the United States. This extension applies to the extent that the United States exercises sovereignty in accordance with international law for the purpose of natural resource exploration and exploitation of such areas. This extension of the definition applies, however, only if the person, property or activity to which the Convention is being applied is connected with such natural resource exploration or exploitation. Thus, it would not include any activity involving the sea floor of an area over which the United States exercised sovereignty for natural resource purposes if that activity was unrelated to the exploration and exploitation of natural resources. This result is consistent with the result that would be obtained under Section 638, which treats the continental shelf as part of the United States for purposes of natural resource exploration and exploitation.

Subparagraph 1(c) defines the term "person" to include an individual, a trust, a partnership, a company and any other body of persons. The definition is significant for a variety of reasons. For example, under Article 4, only a "person" can be a "resident" and therefore eligible for most benefits under the treaty. Also, all "persons" are eligible to claim relief under Article 24 (Mutual Agreement Procedure).

The term "company" is defined in subparagraph 1(d) as a body corporate or an entity treated as a body corporate for tax purposes in the state where it is organized. The definition refers to the law of the state in which an entity is organized in order to ensure that an entity that is treated as fiscally transparent in its country of residence will not get inappropriate benefits, such as the reduced withholding rate provided by subparagraph 2(b) of Article 10 (Dividends). It also ensures that the Limitation on Benefits provisions of Article 21 will be applied at the appropriate level.

Subparagraph 1(e) defines the term "enterprise" as any activity or set of activities that constitutes the carrying on of a business. The term "business" is not defined, but subparagraph (k) provides that it includes the performance of professional services and other activities of an independent character. Both subparagraphs are identical to definitions recently added to the OECD Model in connection with the deletion of Article 14 (Independent Personal Services) from the OECD Model. The inclusion of the two definitions is intended to clarify that income from the performance of professional services or other activities of an independent character is dealt with under Article 7 (Business Profits) and not Article 20 (Other Income).

The terms "enterprise of a Contracting State" and "enterprise of the other Contracting State" are defined in subparagraph 1(f) as an enterprise carried on by a resident of a Contracting State and an enterprise carried on by a resident of the other Contracting State. An enterprise of a Contracting State need not be carried on in that State. It may be carried on in the other Contracting State or a third state (e.g., a U.S. corporation doing all of its business in the other Contracting State would still be a U.S. enterprise). Although not explicitly stated in the Convention, these terms also encompass an enterprise conducted through an entity (such as a partnership) that is treated as fiscally transparent in the Contracting State where the entity's owner is resident. In accordance with Article 4 (Resident), entities that are fiscally transparent in

8

the Contracting State in which their owners are resident are not considered to be residents of that State (although income derived by such entities may be taxed as the income of a resident, if taxed in the hands of resident partners or other owners). An enterprise conducted by such an entity will be treated as carried on by a resident of a Contracting State to the extent its partners or other owners are residents. This approach is consistent with the Code, which under section 875 attributes a trade or business conducted by a partnership to its partners and a trade or business conducted by an estate or trust to its beneficiaries.

Subparagraph 1(g) provides that the terms "a Contracting State" and "the other Contracting State" shall mean Iceland or the United States, as the context requires.

Subparagraph 1(h) defines the term "international traffic." The term means any transport by a ship or aircraft except when such transport is solely between places within a Contracting State. This definition is applicable principally in the context of Article 8 (Shipping and Air Transport). The definition combines with paragraphs 2 and 3 of Article 8 to exempt from tax by the source State income from the rental of ships or aircraft that is earned both by lessors that are operators of ships and aircraft and by those lessors that are not (e.g., a bank or a container leasing company).

The exclusion from international traffic of transport solely between places within a Contracting State means, for example, that carriage of goods or passengers solely between New York and Chicago would not be treated as international traffic, whether carried by a U.S. or a foreign carrier. The substantive taxing rules of the Convention relating to the taxation of income from transport, principally Article 8 (Shipping and Air Transport), therefore, would not apply to income from such carriage. Thus, if the carrier engaged in internal U.S. traffic were a resident of Iceland (assuming that were possible under U.S. law), the United States would not be required to exempt the income from that transport under Article 8. The income would, however, be treated as business profits under Article 7 (Business Profits), and therefore would be taxable in the United States only if attributable to a U.S. permanent establishment of the foreign carrier, and then only on a net basis. The gross basis U.S. tax imposed by section 887 would never apply under the circumstances described. If, however, goods or passengers are carried by a carrier resident in Iceland from a non-U.S. port to, for example, New York, and some of the goods or passengers continue on to Chicago, the entire transport would be international traffic. This would be true if the international carrier transferred the goods at the U.S. port of entry from a ship to a land vehicle, from a ship to a lighter, or even if the overland portion of the trip in the United States was handled by an independent carrier under contract with the original international-al carrier, so long as both parts of the trip were reflected in original bills of lading. For this reason, the Convention, following the U.S. Model, refers in the definition of "international traffic," to "such transport" being solely between places in the other Contracting State, while the OECD Model refers to the ship or aircraft being operated solely between such places. The formulation in the Convention is intended to make clear that, as in the above example, even if the goods are carried on a different aircraft for the internal portion of the international voyage than is used for the overseas portion of the trip, the definition applies to that internal portion as well as the external portion.

Finally, a "cruise to nowhere," i.e., a cruise beginning and ending in a port in the same Contracting State with no stops in a foreign port, would not constitute international traffic.

Subparagraph 1(i) designates the "competent authorities" for Iceland and the United States. In the case of Iceland, the competent authority is the Minister of Finance or his authorized representative. The U.S. competent authority is the Secretary of the Treasury or his delegate. The Secretary of the Treasury has delegated the competent authority function to the Commissioner of Internal Revenue, who in turn has delegated the authority to the Deputy Commissioner (International) LMSB. With respect to interpretative issues, the Deputy Commissioner (International) LMSB acts with the concurrence of the Associate Chief Counsel (International) of the Internal Revenue Service.

The term "national," as it relates to the United States and to Iceland, is defined in subparagraph 1(j). This term is relevant for purposes of Articles 18 (Government Service) and 23 (Non-Discrimination). A national of one of the Contracting States is (1) an individual who is a citizen or national of that State, and (2) any legal person, partnership or association deriving its status, as such, from the law in force in the State where it is established.

Subparagraph 1(l) defines the term "pension scheme" to include any plan, scheme, fund, trust or other arrangement established in a Contracting State that is generally exempt from income taxation in that State and that is operated principally to administer or provide pension or retirement benefits or to earn income for the benefit of one or more such arrangements. Subparagraph 1(b) of the Protocol provides that in the case of the United States, the term "pension scheme" includes the following: a trust providing pension or retirement benefits under a Code section 401(a) qualified pension plan, profit sharing or stock bonus plan, a Code section 403(a) qualified annuity plan, a Code section 403(b) plan, a trust that is an individual retirement account under Code section 408, a Roth individual retirement account under Code section 408A, or a simple retirement account under Code section 408(p), a trust providing pension or retirement benefits under a simplified employee pension plan under Code section 408(k), a trust described in section 457(g) providing pension or retirement benefits under a Code section 457(b) plan, and the Thrift Savings Fund (section 7701(j)). Section 401(k) plans and group trusts described in Revenue Ruling 81-100 and meeting the conditions of Revenue Ruling 2004-67 qualify as pension funds to the extent they are Code section 401(a) plans or other pension schemes. In the case of Iceland, subparagraph 1(a) of the Protocol provides that the term "pension scheme" includes any pension fund or pension plan qualified under the Pension Act or any identical or substantially similar schemes which are created under any law enacted after October 23, 2007, the date of signature of the Convention.

Paragraph 2

Terms that are not defined in the Convention are dealt with in paragraph 2.

Paragraph 2 provides that in the application of the Convention, any term used but not defined in the Convention will have the meaning that it has under the law of the Contracting State whose tax is being applied, unless the context requires otherwise, or the competent authorities have agreed on a different meaning pursuant to Article 24 (Mutual Agreement Procedure). If the term is defined under both the tax and non-tax laws of a Contracting State, the definition in the tax law will take precedence over the definition in the non-tax laws. Finally, there also may be cases where the tax laws of a State contain multiple definitions of the same term. In such a case, the definition used for purposes of the particular provision at issue, if any, should be used.

If the meaning of a term cannot be readily determined under the law of a Contracting State, or if there is a conflict in meaning under the laws of the two States that creates difficulties in the application of the Convention, the competent authorities, as indicated in subparagraph 3(f) of Article 24, may establish a common meaning in order to prevent double taxation or to further any other purpose of the Convention. This common meaning need not conform to the meaning of the term under the laws of either Contracting State.

The reference in paragraph 2 to the internal law of a Contracting State means the law in effect at the time the treaty is being applied, not the law as in effect at the time the treaty was signed. The use of "ambulatory" definitions, however, may lead to results that are at variance with the intentions of the negotiators and of the Contracting States when the treaty was negotiated and ratified. The reference in both paragraphs 1 and 2 to the "context otherwise requir[ing]" a definition different from the treaty definition, in paragraph 1, or from the internal law definition of the Contracting State whose tax is being imposed, under paragraph 2, refers to a circumstance where the result intended by the Contracting States is different from the result that would obtain under either the paragraph 1 definition or the statutory definition. Thus, flexibility in defining terms is necessary and permitted.

ARTICLE 4 (RESIDENT)

This Article sets forth rules for determining whether a person is a resident of a Contracting State for purposes of the Convention. As a general matter only residents of the Contracting States may claim the benefits of the Convention. The treaty definition of residence is to be used only for purposes of the Convention. The fact that a person is determined to be a resident of a Contracting State under Article 4 does not necessarily entitle that person to the benefits of the Convention. In addition to being a resident, a person also must qualify for benefits under Article 21 (Limitation On Benefits) in order to receive benefits conferred on residents of a Contracting State.

The determination of residence for treaty purposes looks first to a person's liability to tax as a resident under the respective taxation laws of the Contracting States. As a general matter, a person who, under those laws, is a resident of one Contracting State and not of the other need look no further. For purposes of the Convention, that person is a resident of the State in which he is resident under internal law. If, however, a person is resident in both Contracting States under their respective taxation laws, the Article proceeds, where possible, to use tie-breaker rules to assign a single State of residence to such a person for purposes of the Convention.

Paragraph 1

The term "resident of a Contracting State" is defined in paragraph 1. In general, this definition incorporates the definitions of residence in U.S. law and that of Iceland by referring to a resident as a person who, under the laws of a Contracting State, is subject to tax there by reason of his domicile, residence, citizenship, place of management, place of incorporation or any other similar criterion. Thus, residents of the United States include aliens who are considered U.S. residents under Code section 7701(b). Paragraph 1 also specifically includes the two Contracting States, and political subdivisions and local authorities of the two States, as residents for purposes of the Convention.

Certain entities that are nominally subject to tax but that in practice are rarely required to pay tax also would generally be treated as residents and therefore accorded treaty benefits. For example, a U.S. Regulated Investment Company (RIC) and a U.S. Real Estate Investment Trust (REIT) are residents of the United States for purposes of the treaty. Although the income earned by these entities normally is not subject to U.S. tax in the hands of the entity, they are taxable to the extent that they do not currently distribute their profits, and therefore may be regarded as "liable to tax." They also must satisfy a number of requirements under the Code in order to be entitled to special tax treatment.

A person who is liable to tax in a Contracting State only in respect of income from sources within that State or capital situated therein or of profits attributable to a permanent establishment in that State will not be treated as a resident of that Contracting State for purposes of the Convention. Thus, a consular official of Iceland who is posted in the United States, who may be subject to U.S. tax on U.S. source investment income but is not taxable in the United States on non-U.S. source income (see Code section 7701(b)(5)(B)), would not be considered a resident of the United States for purposes of the Convention. Similarly, an enterprise of Iceland with a permanent establishment in the United States is not, by virtue of that permanent establishment, a resident of the United States. The enterprise generally is subject to U.S. tax only with respect to its income that is attributable to the U.S. permanent establishment, not with respect to its worldwide income, as it would be if it were a U.S. resident.

Paragraph 2

Paragraph 2 provides that certain tax-exempt entities such as pension schemes and charitable organizations will be regarded as residents of a Contracting State regardless of whether they are generally liable to income tax in the State where they are established. The inclusion of this provision is intended to clarify the generally accepted practice of treating an entity that would be liable for tax as a resident under the internal law of a State but for a specific exemption from tax (either complete or partial) as a resident of that State for purposes of paragraph 1.

Subparagraph 2(a) applies to pension schemes, as defined in subparagraph 1(l) of Article 3 (General Definitions). Subparagraph 2(b) applies to any plan, scheme, fund, trust, company or other arrangement established in a Contracting State that is generally exempt from taxation in that State because it is operated exclusively to administer or provide employee benefits. The reference to a general exemption is intended to reflect the fact that under U.S. law, certain organizations that generally are considered to be tax-exempt entities may be subject to certain excise taxes or to income tax on their unrelated business income. Subparagraph 2(c) applies to an organization that is established exclusively for religious, charitable, scientific, artistic, cultural, or educational purposes and that is a resident of a Contracting State. Thus, a section 501(c) organization organized in the United States (such as a U.S. charity) that is generally exempt from tax under U.S. law is a resident of the United States for all purposes of the Convention.

Paragraph 3

If, under the laws of the two Contracting States, and, thus, under paragraph 1, an individual is deemed to be a resident of both Contracting States, a series of tie-breaker rules are provided in paragraph 3 to determine a single State of residence for that individual. These tests are to be applied in the order in which they are stated. The first test is based on where the individual has a permanent home. If that test is inconclusive because the individual has a permanent home available to him in both States, he will be considered to be a resident of the Contracting State where his personal and economic relations are closest (i.e., the location of his "center of vital interests"). If that test is also inconclusive, or if he does not have a permanent home available to him in either State, he will be treated as a resident of the Contracting State where he maintains a habitual abode. If he has a habitual abode in both States or in neither of them, he will be treated as a resident of the Contracting State of which he is a national. If he is a national of both States or of neither, the matter will be considered by the competent authorities, who will assign a single State of residence.

Paragraph 4

Paragraph 4 seeks to settle dual residence issues for persons other than individuals (e.g., companies, trusts, or estates). For example, a dual residence may arise in the case of a company that is dually created in both the United States and Iceland or that is incorporated in the United States, and therefore treated as a resident of the United States, but that is also considered a resident of Iceland because it is managed and controlled in Iceland. In such a case, if such a person is, under the rules of paragraph 1, resident in both Contracting States, the competent authorities shall seek to determine a single State of residence for that person for purposes of the Convention. If the competent authorities do not reach an agreement on a single State of residence, that company may not claim any benefit accorded to residents of a Contracting State by the Convention, except those provided in Article 23 (Non-Discrimination) and Article 24 (Mutual Agreement Procedure). Thus, for example, a State cannot impose discriminatory tax measures on a dual resident company.

Dual resident companies may be treated as a resident of a Contracting State for purposes other than that of obtaining benefits under the Convention. For example, if a dual resident company pays a dividend to a resident of Iceland, the U.S. paying agent would withhold on that dividend at the appropriate treaty rate because reduced withholding is a benefit enjoyed by the resident of Iceland, not by the dual resident company. The dual resident company that paid the dividend would, for this purpose, be treated as a resident of the United States under the Convention. In addition, information relating to dual resident companies can be exchanged under the Convention because, by its terms, Article 26 (Exchange of Information and Administrative Assistance) is not limited to residents of the Contracting States.

ARTICLE 5 (PERMANENT ESTABLISHMENT)

This Article defines the term "permanent establishment," a term that is significant for several articles of the Convention. The existence of a permanent establishment in a Contracting State is necessary under Article 7 (Business Profits) for the taxation by that State of the business profits of a resident of the other Contracting State. Articles 10 (Dividends), 11 (Interest) and 12 (Royalties) provide for reduced rates of tax at source on payments of these items of income to a resident of the other State only when the income is not attributable to a permanent establishment that the recipient has in the source State. The concept is also relevant in determining which Contracting State may tax certain gains under Article 13 (Capital Gains) and certain "other income" under Article 20 (Other Income).

Paragraph 1

The basic definition of the term "permanent establishment" is contained in paragraph 1. As used in the Convention, the term means a fixed place of business through which the business of an enterprise is wholly or partly carried on. As indicated in the OECD Commentary to Article 5 (see paragraphs 4 through 8), a general principle to be observed in determining whether a permanent establishment exists is that the place of business must be "fixed" in the sense that a particular building or physical location is used by the enterprise for the conduct of its business, and that it must be foreseeable that the enterprise's use of this building or other physical location will be more than temporary.

Paragraph 2

Paragraph 2 lists a number of types of fixed places of business that constitute a permanent establishment. This list is illustrative and non-exclusive. According to paragraph 2, the term permanent establishment includes a place of management, a branch, an office, a factory, a workshop, and a mine, oil or gas well, quarry or other place of extraction of natural resources.

Paragraph 3

This paragraph provides rules to determine whether a building site or a construction, assembly or installation project, or an installation or drilling rig or ship used for the exploration of natural resources constitutes a permanent establishment for the contractor, driller, etc. Such a site or activity does not create a permanent establishment unless the site, project, etc. lasts, or the exploration activity continues, for more than twelve months. It is only necessary to refer to "exploration" and not "exploitation" in this context because exploitation activities are defined to constitute a permanent establishment under subparagraph 2(f). Thus, a drilling rig does not constitute a permanent establishment if a well is drilled in only six months, but if production begins in the following month the well becomes a permanent establishment as of that date.

The twelve-month test applies separately to each site or project. The twelve-month period begins when work (including preparatory work carried on by the enterprise) physically begins in a Contracting State. A series of contracts or projects by a contractor that are interdependent both commercially and geographically are to be treated as a single project for purposes of applying the twelve-month threshold test. For example, the construction of a housing development would be considered as a single project even if each house were constructed for a different purchaser.

In applying this paragraph, time spent by a sub-contractor on a building site is counted as time spent by the general contractor at the site for purposes of determining whether the general contractor has a permanent establishment. However, for the sub-contractor itself to be treated as having a permanent establishment, the sub-contractor's activities at the site must last for more than 12 months. If a sub-contractor is on a site intermittently, then, for purposes of applying the 12-month rule, time is measured from the first day the sub-contractor is on the site until the last day (*i.e.*, intervening days that the sub-contractor is not on the site are counted).

These interpretations of the Article are based on the Commentary to paragraph 3 of Article 5 of the OECD Model, which contains language that is substantially the same as that in the Convention. These interpretations are consistent with the generally accepted international interpretation of the relevant language in paragraph 3 of Article 5 of the Convention.

If the twelve-month threshold is exceeded, the site or project constitutes a permanent establishment from the first day of activity.

Paragraph 4

This paragraph contains exceptions to the general rule of paragraph 1, listing a number of activities that may be carried on through a fixed place of business but which nevertheless do not create a permanent establishment. The use of facilities solely to store, display or deliver merchandise belonging to an enterprise does not constitute a permanent establishment of that enterprise. The maintenance of a stock of goods belonging to an enterprise solely for the purpose of storage, display or delivery, or solely for the purpose of processing by another enterprise does not give rise to a permanent establishment of the first-mentioned enterprise. The maintenance of a fixed place of business solely for the purpose of purchasing goods or merchandise, or for collecting information, for the enterprise, or for other activities that have a preparatory or auxiliary character for the enterprise, such as advertising, or the supply of information, do not constitute a permanent establishment of the enterprise. Moreover, subparagraph 4(f) provides that a combination of the activities described in the other subparagraphs of paragraph 4 will not give rise to a permanent establishment if the combination results in an overall activity that is of a preparatory or auxiliary character.

Paragraph 5

Paragraphs 5 and 6 specify when activities carried on by an agent or other person acting on behalf of an enterprise create a permanent establishment of that enterprise. Under paragraph 5, a person is deemed to create a permanent establishment of the enterprise if that person has and habitually exercises an authority to conclude contracts in the name of the enterprise. If, however, for example, his activities are limited to those activities specified in paragraph 4 which would not constitute a permanent establishment if carried on by the enterprise through a fixed place of business, the person does not create a permanent establishment of the enterprise.

The Convention adopts the OECD Model language "in the name of the enterprise " rather than the U.S. Model language "binding on the enterprise." This difference in language is not intended to be a substantive difference. As indicated in paragraph 32 to the OECD Commentaries on Article 5, paragraph 5 is intended to encompass persons who have "sufficient authority to bind the enterprise's participation in the business activity in the State concerned."

The contracts referred to in paragraph 5 are those relating to the essential business operations of the enterprise, rather than ancillary activities. For example, if the person has no authority to conclude contracts in the name of the enterprise with its customers for, say, the sale of the goods produced by the enterprise, but it can enter into service contracts in the name of the enterprise for the enterprise's business equipment, this contracting authority would not fall within the scope of the paragraph, even if exercised regularly.

Paragraph 6

Under paragraph 6, an enterprise is not deemed to have a permanent establishment in a Contracting State merely because it carries on business in that State through an independent agent, including a broker or general commission agent, if the agent is acting in the ordinary course of his business as an independent agent. Thus, there are two conditions that must be satisfied: the agent must be both legally and economically independent of the enterprise, and the agent must be acting in the ordinary course of its business in carrying out activities on behalf of the enterprise.

Whether the agent and the enterprise are independent is a factual determination. Among the questions to be considered are the extent to which the agent operates on the basis of instructions from the enterprise. An agent that is subject to detailed instructions regarding the conduct of its operations or comprehensive control by the enterprise is not legally independent.

In determining whether the agent is economically independent, a relevant factor is the extent to which the agent bears business risk. Business risk refers primarily to risk of loss. An independent agent typically bears risk of loss from its own activities. In the absence of other factors that would establish dependence, an agent that shares business risk with the enterprise, or has its own business risk, is economically independent because its business activities are not integrated with those of the principal. Conversely, an agent that bears little or no risk from the activities it performs is not economically independent and therefore is not described in paragraph 6.

Another relevant factor in determining whether an agent is economically independent is whether the agent acts exclusively or nearly exclusively for the principal. Such a relationship may indicate that the principal has economic control over the agent. A number of principals acting in concert also may have economic control over an agent. The limited scope of the agent's activities and the agent's dependence on a single source of income may indicate that the agent lacks economic independence. It should be borne in mind, however, that exclusivity is not in itself a conclusive test; an agent may be economically independent notwithstanding an exclusive relationship with the principal if it has the capacity to diversify and acquire other clients without substantial modifications to its current business and without substantial harm to its business profits. Thus, exclusivity should be viewed merely as a pointer to further investigation of the relationship between the principal and the agent. Each case must be addressed on the basis of its own facts and circumstances.

Paragraph 7

This paragraph clarifies that a company that is a resident of a Contracting State is not deemed to have a permanent establishment in the other Contracting State merely because it controls, or is controlled by, a company that is a resident of that other Contracting State, or that carries on business in that other Contracting State. The determination whether a permanent establishment exists is made solely on the basis of the factors described in paragraphs 1 through 6 of the Article. Whether a company is a permanent establishment of a related company, therefore, is based solely on those factors and not on the ownership or control relationship between the companies.

ARTICLE 6 (INCOME FROM IMMOVABLE PROPERTY (REAL PROPERTY))

This Article deals with the taxation of income from immovable property (real property) situated in a Contracting State (the "situs State"). The Article does not grant an exclusive taxing right to the situs State; the situs State is merely given the primary right to tax. The Article does not impose any limitation in terms of rate or form of tax imposed by the situs State.

Paragraph 1

The first paragraph of Article 6 states the general rule that income of a resident of a Contracting State derived from real property situated in the other Contracting State may be taxed in the Contracting State in which the property is situated. The paragraph specifies that income from real property includes income from agriculture and forestry.

Paragraph 2

The term "real property" is defined in paragraph 2 by reference to the internal law definition in the situs State. In the case of the United States, the term has the meaning given to it by Reg. § 1.897-1(b). In addition to the statutory definitions in the two Contracting States, the paragraph specifies certain additional classes of property that, regardless of internal law definitions, are within the scope of the term for purposes of the Convention. This expanded definition conforms to that in the OECD Model. The definition of "real property" for purposes of Article 6 is more limited than the expansive definition of "real property" in paragraph 1 of Article 13 (Capital Gains). The Article 13 term includes not only real property as defined in Article 6 but certain other interests in real property.

Paragraph 3

Paragraph 3 makes clear that all forms of income derived from the exploitation of real property are taxable in the Contracting State in which the property is situated. This includes income from any use of real property, including, but not limited to, income from direct use by the owner (in which case income may be imputed to the owner for tax purposes) and rental income from the letting of real property. In the case of a net lease of real property, if any elections to be taxed on a net basis as may be provided under the laws of the situs State have not been made, the gross rental payment (before deductible expenses incurred by the lessee) is treated as income from the property.

Other income closely associated with real property is covered by other Articles of the Convention, however, and not Article 6. For example, income from the disposition of an interest in real property is not considered "derived" from real property; taxation of that income is addressed in Article 13. Interest paid on a mortgage on real property would be covered by Article 11 (Interest). Distributions by a U.S. Real Estate Investment Trust or certain regulated investment companies would fall under Article 13 in the case of distributions of U.S. real property gain or Article 10 (Dividends) in the case of distributions treated as dividends. Finally, distributions from a United States Real Property Holding Corporation are not considered to be income from the exploitation of real property; such payments would fall under Article 10 or 13.

Paragraph 4

This paragraph specifies that the basic rule of paragraph 1 (as elaborated in paragraph 3) applies to income from real property of an enterprise. This clarifies that the situs country may tax the real property income (including rental income) of a resident of the other Contracting State in the absence of attribution to a permanent establishment in the situs State. This provision represents an exception to the general rule under Articles 7 (Business Profits) that income must be attributable to a permanent establishment in order to be taxable in the situs State.

ARTICLE 7 (BUSINESS PROFITS)

This Article provides rules for the taxation by a Contracting State of the business profits of an enterprise of the other Contracting State.

Paragraph 1

Paragraph 1 states the general rule that business profits of an enterprise of one Contracting State may not be taxed by the other Contracting State unless the enterprise carries on business in that other Contracting State through a permanent establishment (as defined in Article 5 (Permanent Establishment)) situated there. When that condition is met, the State in which the permanent establishment is situated may tax the enterprise on the income that is attributable to the permanent establishment.

Although the Convention does not include a definition of "business profits," the term is intended to cover income derived from any trade or business. In accordance with this broad definition, the term "business profits" includes income attributable to notional principal contracts and other financial instruments to the extent that the income is attributable to a trade or business of dealing in such instruments or is otherwise related to a trade or business (as in the case of a notional principal contract entered into for the purpose of hedging currency risk arising from an active trade or business). Any other income derived from such instruments is, unless specifically covered in another article, dealt with under Article 20 (Other Income).

The term "business profits" also includes income derived by an enterprise from the rental of tangible personal property (unless such tangible personal property consists of aircraft, ships or containers, income from which is addressed by Article 8 (Shipping and Air Transport)). The inclusion of income derived by an enterprise from the rental of tangible personal property in business profits means that such income earned by a resident of a Contracting State can be taxed by the other Contracting State only if the income is attributable to a permanent establishment maintained by the resident in that other State, and, if the income is taxable, it can be taxed only on a net basis. Income from the rental of tangible personal property that is not derived in connection with a trade or business is dealt with in Article 20.

In addition, as a result of the definitions of "enterprise" and "business" in Article 3 (General Definitions), the term includes income derived from the furnishing of personal services. Thus, a consulting firm resident in one State whose employees or partners perform services in the other State through a permanent establishment may be taxed in that other State on a net basis under Article 7, and not under Article 14 (Income from Employment), which applies only to income of employees. With respect to the enterprise's employees themselves, however, their salary remains subject to Article 14.

Because this Article applies to income earned by an enterprise from the furnishing of personal services, the Article also applies to income derived by a partner resident in a Contracting State that is attributable to personal services performed in the other Contracting State through a partnership with a permanent establishment in that other State. Income which may be taxed under this Article includes all income attributable to the permanent establishment in respect of the performance of the personal services carried on by the partnership (whether by the partner himself, other partners in the partnership, or by employees assisting the partners) and any income from activities ancillary to the performance of those services (*e.g.*, charges for facsimile services).

The application of Article 7 to a service partnership may be illustrated by the following example: a partnership has five partners (who agree to split profits equally), four of whom are resident and perform personal services only in Iceland at Office A, and one of whom performs personal services at Office B, a permanent establishment in the United States. In this case, the four partners of the partnership resident in Iceland may be taxed in the United States in respect of their share of the income attributable to the permanent establishment, Office B. The services giving rise to income which may be attributed to the permanent establishment would include not only the services performed by the one resident partner, but also, for example, if one of the four other partners came to the United States and worked on an Office B matter there, the income in respect of those services. Income from the services performed by the visiting partner would be subject to tax in the United States regardless of whether the visiting partner actually visited or used Office B while performing services in the United States.

Paragraph 2

Paragraph 2 provides rules for the attribution of business profits to a permanent establishment. The Contracting States will attribute to a permanent establishment the profits that it would have earned had it been a distinct and separate enterprise engaged in the same or similar activities under the same or similar conditions and dealing wholly independently with the enterprise of which it is a permanent establishment.

The "attributable to" concept of paragraph 2 provides an alternative to the analogous but somewhat different "effectively connected" concept in Code section 864(c). Depending on the circumstances, the amount of income "attributable to" a permanent establishment under Article 7 may be greater or less than the amount of income that would be treated as "effectively connected" to a U.S. trade or business under Code section 864. In particular, in the case of financial institutions, the use of internal dealings to allocate income within an enterprise may produce results under Article 7 that are significantly different than the results under the effectively connected income rules. For example, income from interbranch notional principal contracts may be taken into account under Article 7, notwithstanding that such transactions may be ignored for purposes of U.S. domestic law.

The profits attributable to a permanent establishment may be from sources within or without a Contracting State. However, the business profits attributable to a permanent establishment include only those profits derived from the assets used, risks assumed, and activities performed by the permanent establishment.

Paragraph 2 of the Protocol confirms that the arm's length method of paragraphs 2 and 3 consists of applying the OECD Transfer Pricing Guidelines, but taking into account the different economic and legal circumstances of a single legal entity (as opposed to separate but associated enterprises). Thus, any of the methods used in the Transfer Pricing Guidelines, including profits methods, may be used as appropriate and in accordance with the Transfer Pricing Guidelines. However, the use of the Transfer Pricing Guidelines applies only for purposes of attributing profits within the legal entity. It does not create legal obligations or other tax consequences that would result from transactions having independent legal significance.

One example of the different circumstances of a single legal entity is that an entity that operates through branches rather than separate subsidiaries generally will have lower capital requirements because all of the assets of the entity are available to support all of the entity's liabilities (with some exceptions attributable to local regulatory restrictions). This is the reason that most commercial banks and some insurance companies operate through branches rather than subsidiaries. The benefit that comes from such lower capital costs must be allocated among the branches in an appropriate manner. This issue does not arise in the case of an enterprise that operates through separate entities, since each entity will have to be separately capitalized or will have to compensate another entity for providing capital (usually through a guarantee).

Under U.S. domestic regulations, internal "transactions" generally are not recognized because they do not have legal significance. In contrast, the Convention provides that such internal dealings may be used to attribute income to a permanent establishment in cases where the dealings accurately reflect the allocation of risk within the enterprise. One example is that of global trading in securities. In many cases, banks use internal swap transactions to transfer risk from one branch to a central location where traders have the expertise to manage that particular type of risk. Under the Convention, such a bank may also use such swap transactions as a means

19

of attributing income between the branches, if use of that method is the "best method" within the meaning of regulation section 1.482-1(c). The books of a branch will not be respected, however, when the results are inconsistent with a functional analysis. So, for example, income from a transaction that is booked in a particular branch (or home office) will not be treated as attributable to that location if the sales and risk management functions that generate the income are performed in another location.

Because the use of profits methods is permissible under paragraph 2, it is not necessary for the Convention to include a provision corresponding to paragraph 4 of Article 7 of the OECD Model.

Paragraph 3

Paragraph 3 provides that in determining the business profits of a permanent establishment, deductions shall be allowed for the expenses incurred for the purposes of the permanent establishment, ensuring that business profits will be taxed on a net basis. This rule is not limited to expenses incurred exclusively for the purposes of the permanent establishment, but includes expenses incurred for the purposes of the enterprise as a whole, or that part of the enterprise that includes the permanent establishment. Deductions are to be allowed regardless of which accounting unit of the enterprise books the expenses, so long as they are incurred for the purposes of the permanent establishment. For example, a portion of the interest expense recorded on the books of the home office in one State may be deducted by a permanent establishment in the other. The amount of the expense that must be allowed as a deduction is determined by applying the arm's length principle. And, as noted above with respect to paragraph 2 of Article 1 (General Scope), if a deduction would be allowed under the Code in computing the U.S. taxable income, the deduction also is allowed in computing taxable income under the Convention. However, except where the Convention provides for more favorable treatment, a taxpayer cannot take deductions for expenses in computing taxable income under the Convention to a greater extent than would be allowed under the Code where doing so would be inconsistent with the intent of the Code. For example, assume that a Bulgarian taxpayer with a permanent establishment in the United States borrows $100 to purchase U.S. tax exempt bonds, and that the $100 of tax-exempt bonds and the $100 of related debt would be treated as assets and liabilities of the permanent establishment. For purposes of computing the profits attributable to the permanent establishment under the Convention, both the tax exempt interest from the bonds and the interest expense from the related debt would be excluded.

As noted above, paragraph the Convention provides that the OECD Transfer Pricing Guidelines apply, by analogy, in determining the profits attributable to a permanent establishment. Accordingly, a permanent establishment may deduct payments made to its head office or another branch in compensation for services performed for the benefit of the branch. The method to be used in calculating that amount will depend on the terms of the arrangements between the branches and head office. For example, the enterprise could have a policy, expressed in writing, under which each business unit could use the services of lawyers employed by the head office. At the end of each year, the costs of employing the lawyers would be charged to each business unit according to the amount of services used by that business unit during the year. Since this appears to be a kind of cost-sharing arrangement and the allocation of costs is based on the benefits received by each business unit, such a cost allocation would be an acceptable means of determining a permanent establishment's deduction for legal expenses. Alternatively, the head office could agree to employ lawyers at its own risk, and to charge an arm's length price for legal services performed for a particular business unit. If the lawyers were under-utilized, and the "fees" received from the business units were less than the cost of employing the lawyers, then the head office would bear the excess cost. If the "fees" exceeded the cost of employing the lawyers, then the head office would keep the excess to compensate it for assuming the risk of employing the lawyers. If the enterprise acted in accordance with this agreement, this method would be an acceptable alternative method for calculating a permanent establishment's deduction for legal expenses.

A permanent establishment cannot be funded entirely with debt, but must have sufficient capital to carry on its activities as if it were a distinct and separate enterprise. To the extent that the permanent establishment has not been attributed capital for profit attribution purposes, a Contracting State may attribute such capital to the permanent establishment, in accordance with the arm's length principle, and deny an interest deduction to the extent necessary to reflect that capital attribution. The method prescribed by U.S. domestic law for making this attribution is found in Treas. Reg. section 1.882-5. Both section 1.882-5 and the method prescribed the Convention start from the premise that all of the capital of the enterprise supports all of the assets and risks of the enterprise, and therefore the entire capital of the enterprise must be allocated to its various businesses and offices.

However, section 1.882-5 does not take into account the fact that some assets create more risk for the enterprise than do other assets. An independent enterprise would need less capital to support a perfectly-hedged U.S. Treasury security than it would need to support an equity security or other asset with significant market and/or credit risk. Accordingly, in some cases section 1.882-5 would require a taxpayer to allocate more capital to the United States, and therefore would reduce the taxpayer's interest deduction more, than is appropriate. To address these cases, the Convention allows a taxpayer to apply a more flexible approach that takes into account the relative risk of its assets in the various jurisdictions in which it does business. In particular, in the case of financial institutions other than insurance companies, the amount of capital attributable to a permanent establishment is determined by allocating the institution's total equity between its various offices on the basis of the proportion of the financial institution's risk-weighted assets attributable to each of them. This recognizes the fact that financial institutions are in many cases required to risk-weight their assets for regulatory purposes and, in other cases, will do so for business reasons even if not required to do so by regulators. However, risk-weighting is more complicated than the method prescribed by section 1.882-5. Accordingly, to ease this administrative burden, taxpayers may choose to apply the principles of Treas. Reg. section 1.882-5(c) to determine the amount of capital allocable to its U.S. permanent establishment, in lieu of determining its allocable capital under the risk-weighted capital allocation method provided by the Convention, even if it has otherwise chosen the principles of Article 7 rather than the effectively connected income rules of U.S. domestic law.

Paragraph 4

Paragraph 4 provides that no business profits can be attributed to a permanent establishment merely because it purchases goods or merchandise for the enterprise of which it is a part. This paragraph is essentially identical to paragraph 5 of Article 7 of the OECD Model. This rule applies only to an office that performs functions for the enterprise in addition to purchasing. The income attribution issue does not arise if the sole activity of the office is the purchase of goods or merchandise because such activity does not give rise to a permanent establishment under Article 5 (Permanent Establishment). A common situation in which paragraph 4 is relevant is one in which a permanent establishment purchases raw materials for the enterprise's manufacturing operation conducted outside the United States and sells the manu-factured product. While business profits may be attributable to the permanent establishment with respect to its sales activities, no profits are attributable to it with respect to its purchasing activities.

Paragraph 5

Paragraph 5 provides that profits shall be determined by the same method each year, unless there is good reason to change the method used. This rule assures consistent tax treatment over time for permanent establishments. It limits the ability of both the Contracting State and the enterprise to change accounting methods to be applied to the permanent establishment. It does not, however, restrict a Contracting State from imposing additional requirements, such as the rules under Code section 481, to prevent amounts from being duplicated or omitted following a change in accounting method. Such adjustments may be necessary, for example, if the taxpayer switches from using the domestic rules under section 864 in one year to using the rules of Article 7 in the next. Also, if the taxpayer switches from Convention-based rules to U.S. domestic rules, it may need to meet certain deadlines for making elections that are not necessary when applying the rules of the Convention.

Paragraph 6

Paragraph 6 coordinates the provisions of Article 7 and other provisions of the Convention. Under this paragraph, when business profits include items of income that are dealt with separately under other articles of the Convention, the provisions of those articles will, except when they specifically provide to the contrary, take precedence over the provisions of Article 7. For example, the taxation of dividends will be determined by the rules of Article 10 (Dividends), and not by Article 7, except where, as provided in paragraph 6 of Article 10, the dividend is attributable to a permanent establishment. In the latter case the provisions of Article 7 apply. Thus, an enterprise of one State deriving dividends from the other State may not rely on Article 7 to exempt those dividends from tax at source if they are not attributable to a permanent establishment of the enterprise in the other State. By the same token, if the dividends are attributable to a permanent establishment in the other State, the dividends may be taxed on a net income basis at the source State full corporate tax rate, rather than on a gross basis under Article 10.

As provided in Article 8 (Shipping and Air Transport), income derived from shipping and air transport activities in international traffic described in that Article is taxable only in the country of residence of the enterprise regardless of whether it is attributable to a permanent establishment situated in the source State.

Paragraph 7

Paragraph 7 incorporates into the Convention the rule of Code section 864(c)(6). Like the Code section on which it is based, paragraph 7 provides that any income or gain attributable to a permanent establishment during its existence is taxable in the Contracting State where the permanent establishment is situated, even if the payment of that income or gain is deferred until after the permanent establishment ceases to exist. This rule applies with respect to paragraphs 1 and 2 of Article 7 (Business Profits), paragraph 6 of Article 10, paragraph 4 of Article 11 (Interest), paragraph 3 of Articles 12 (Royalties) and 13 (Capital Gains) and paragraph 2 of Article 20 (Other Income).

The effect of this rule can be illustrated by the following example. Assume a company that is a resident of Iceland and that maintains a permanent establishment in the United States winds up the permanent establishment's business and sells the permanent establishment's inventory and assets to a U.S. buyer at the end of year 1 in exchange for an interest-bearing installment obligation payable in full at the end of year 3. Despite the fact that Article 13's threshold requirement for U.S. taxation is not met in year 3 because the company has no permanent establishment in the United States, the United States may tax the deferred income payment recognized by the company in year 3.

Relationship to Other Articles

This Article is subject to the saving clause of paragraph 4 of Article 1 (General Scope) of the Model. Thus, if a citizen of the United States who is a resident of Iceland under the treaty derives business profits from the United States that are not attributable to a permanent establishment in the United States, the United States may, subject to the special foreign tax credit rules of paragraph 4 of Article 22 (Relief from Double Taxation), tax those profits, notwithstanding the provision of paragraph 1 of this Article which would exempt the income from U.S. tax.

The benefits of this Article are also subject to Article 21 (Limitation on Benefits). Thus, an enterprise of Iceland that derives income effectively connected with a U.S. trade or business may not claim the benefits of Article 7 unless the resident carrying on the enterprise qualifies for such benefits under Article 21.

As provided in paragraph 3 of the Protocol, Articles 7 and 23 (Non-Discrimination) shall not prevent Iceland from continuing to tax permanent establishments of United States insurance companies in accordance with Article 70, paragraph 2, section 3 of the Icelandic Tax Code, nor shall it prevent the United States from continuing to tax permanent establishments of Icelandic insurance companies in accordance with section 842 b) of the Code.

ARTICLE 8 (SHIPPING AND AIR TRANSPORT)

This Article governs the taxation of profits from the operation of ships and aircraft in international traffic. The term "international traffic" is defined in subparagraph 1(h) of Article 3 (General Definitions).

Paragraph 1

Paragraph 1 provides that profits derived by an enterprise of a Contracting State from the operation in international traffic of ships or aircraft are taxable only in that Contracting State. Because paragraph 6 of Article 7 (Business Profits) defers to Article 8 with respect to shipping income, such income derived by a resident of one of the Contracting States may not be taxed in the other State even if the enterprise has a permanent establishment in that other State. Thus, if a U.S. airline has a ticket office in Iceland, Iceland may not tax the airline's profits attributable to that office under Article 7. Since entities engaged in international transportation activities normally will have many permanent establishments in a number of countries, the rule avoids difficulties that would be encountered in attributing income to multiple permanent establishments if the income were covered by Article 7.

Paragraph 2

The income from the operation of ships or aircraft in international traffic that is exempt from tax under paragraph 1 is defined in paragraph 2.

In addition to income derived directly from the operation of ships and aircraft in international traffic, this definition also includes certain items of rental income. First, income of an enterprise of a Contracting State from the rental of ships or aircraft on a full basis (i.e., with crew) is income of the lessor from the operation of ships and aircraft in international traffic and, therefore, is exempt from tax in the other Contracting State under paragraph 1. Also, paragraph 2 encompasses income from the lease of ships or aircraft on a bareboat basis (i.e., without crew), either when the income is incidental to other income of the lessor from the operation of ships or aircraft in international traffic, or when the ships or aircraft are operated in international traffic by the lessee. If neither of those two conditions apply, income from the bareboat rentals would constitute business profits. The coverage of Article 8 is therefore broader than that of Article 8 of the OECD Model, which covers bareboat leasing only when it is incidental to other income of the lessor from the operation of ships of aircraft in international traffic.

Paragraph 2 also clarifies, consistent with the Commentary to Article 8 of the OECD Model, that income earned by an enterprise from the inland transport of property or passengers within either Contracting State falls within Article 8 if the transport is undertaken as part of the international transport of property or passengers by the enterprise. Thus, if a U.S. shipping company contracts to carry property from Iceland to a U.S. city and, as part of that contract, it transports the property by truck from its point of origin to an airport in Iceland (or it contracts with a trucking company to carry the property to the airport) the income earned by the U.S. shipping company from the overland leg of the journey would be taxable only in the United States. Similarly, Article 8 also would apply to all of the income derived from a contract for the international transport of goods, even if the goods were transported to the port by a lighter, not by the vessel that carried the goods in international waters.

Finally, certain non-transport activities that are an integral part of the services performed by a transport company, or are ancillary to the enterprise's operation of ships or aircraft in international traffic, are understood to be covered in paragraph 1, though they are not specified in paragraph 2. These include, for example, the provision of goods and services by engineers, ground and equipment maintenance and staff, cargo handlers, catering staff and customer services personnel. Where the enterprise provides such goods to, or performs services for, other enterprises and such activities are directly connected with or ancillary to the enterprise's operation of ships or aircraft in international traffic, the profits from the provision of such goods and services to other enterprises will fall under this paragraph.

For example, enterprises engaged in the operation of ships or aircraft in international traffic may enter into pooling arrangements for the purposes of reducing the costs of maintaining facilities needed for the operation of their ships or aircraft in other countries. For instance, where an airline enterprise agrees (for example, under an International Airlines Technical Pool agreement) to provide spare parts or maintenance services to other airlines landing at a particular location (which allows it to benefit from these services at other locations), activities carried on pursuant to that agreement will be ancillary to the operation of aircraft in international traffic by the enterprise.

Also, advertising that the enterprise may do for other enterprises in magazines offered aboard ships or aircraft that it operates in international traffic or at its business locations, such as ticket offices, is ancillary to its operation of these ships or aircraft. Profits generated by such advertising fall within this paragraph. Income earned by concessionaires, however, is not covered by Article 8. These interpretations of paragraph 1 also are consistent with the Commentary to Article 8 of the OECD Model.

Paragraph 3

Under this paragraph, profits of an enterprise of a Contracting State from the use, maintenance or rental of containers (including equipment for their transport) used in international traffic are exempt from tax in the other Contracting State. This result obtains under paragraph 3 regardless of whether the recipient of the income is engaged in the operation of ships or aircraft in international traffic, and regardless of whether the enterprise has a permanent establishment in the other Contracting State. Only income from the use, maintenance or rental of containers that is incidental to other income from international traffic is covered by Article 8 of the OECD Model.

Paragraph 4

This paragraph clarifies that the provisions of paragraphs 1 and 3 also apply to profits derived by an enterprise of a Contracting State from participation in a pool, joint business or international operating agency. This refers to various arrangements for international cooperation by carriers in shipping and air transport. For example, airlines from two countries may agree to share the transport of passengers between the two countries. They each will fly the same number of flights per week and share the revenues from that route equally, regardless of the number of passengers that each airline actually transports. Paragraph 4 makes clear that with respect to each carrier the income dealt with in the Article is that carrier's share of the total transport, not the income derived from the passengers actually carried by the airline. This paragraph corresponds to paragraph 4 of Article 8 of the OECD Model.

Relationship to Other Articles

The taxation of gains from the alienation of ships, aircraft or containers is not dealt with in this Article but in paragraph 4 of Article 13 (Capital Gains).

As with other benefits of the Convention, the benefit of exclusive residence country taxation under Article 8 is available to an enterprise only if it is entitled to benefits under Article 21 (Limitation on Benefits).

This Article also is subject to the saving clause of paragraph 4 of Article 1 (General Scope) of the Model. Thus, if a citizen of the United States who is a resident of Iceland derives profits from the operation of ships or aircraft in international traffic, notwithstanding the exclusive residence country taxation in paragraph 1 of Article 8, the United States may, subject to the special foreign tax credit rules of paragraph 4 of Article 22 (Relief from Double Taxation), tax those profits as part of the worldwide income of the citizen. (This is an unlikely situation,

however, because non-tax considerations (e.g., insurance) generally result in shipping activities being carried on in corporate form.)

ARTICLE 9 (ASSOCIATED ENTERPRISES)

This Article incorporates in the Convention the arm's-length principle reflected in the U.S. domestic transfer pricing provisions, particularly Code section 482. It provides that when related enterprises engage in a transaction on terms that are not arm's-length, the Contracting States may make appropriate adjustments to the taxable income and tax liability of such related enterprises to reflect what the income and tax of these enterprises with respect to the transaction would have been had there been an arm's-length relationship between them.

Paragraph 1

This paragraph is essentially the same as its counterpart in the U.S. and OECD Models. It addresses the situation where an enterprise of a Contracting State is related to an enterprise of the other Contracting State, and there are arrangements or conditions imposed between the enterprises in their commercial or financial relations that are different from those that would have existed in the absence of the relationship. Under these circumstances, the Contracting States may adjust the income (or loss) of the enterprise to reflect what it would have been in the absence of such a relationship.

The paragraph identifies the relationships between enterprises that serve as a prerequisite to application of the Article. As the Commentary to the OECD Model makes clear, the necessary element in these relationships is effective control, which is also the standard for purposes of section 482. Thus, the Article applies if an enterprise of one State participates directly or indirectly in the management, control, or capital of the enterprise of the other State. Also, the Article applies if any third person or persons participate directly or indirectly in the management, control, or capital of enterprises of different States. For this purpose, all types of control are included, i.e., whether or not legally enforceable and however exercised or exercisable.

The fact that a transaction is entered into between such related enterprises does not, in and of itself, mean that a Contracting State may adjust the income (or loss) of one or both of the enterprises under the provisions of this Article. If the conditions of the transaction are consistent with those that would be made between independent persons, the income arising from that transaction should not be subject to adjustment under this Article.

Similarly, the fact that associated enterprises may have concluded arrangements, such as cost sharing arrangements or general services agreements, is not in itself an indication that the two enterprises have entered into a non-arm's-length transaction that should give rise to an adjustment under paragraph 1. Both related and unrelated parties enter into such arrangements (e.g., joint venturers may share some development costs). As with any other kind of transaction, when related parties enter into an arrangement, the specific arrangement must be examined to see whether or not it meets the arm's-length standard. In the event that it does not, an appropriate adjustment may be made, which may include modifying the terms of the agreement or re-characterizing the transaction to reflect its substance.

It is understood that the "commensurate with income" standard for determining appropriate transfer prices for intangibles, added to Code section 482 by the Tax Reform Act of 1986, was designed to operate consistently with the arm's-length standard. The implementation of this standard in the section 482 regulations is in accordance with the general principles of paragraph 1 of Article 9 of the Convention, as interpreted by the OECD Transfer Pricing Guidelines.

This Article also permits tax authorities to deal with thin capitalization issues. They may, in the context of Article 9, scrutinize more than the rate of interest charged on a loan between related persons. They also may examine the capital structure of an enterprise, whether a payment in respect of that loan should be treated as interest, and, if it is treated as interest, under what circumstances interest deductions should be allowed to the payor. Paragraph 2 of the Commentary to Article 9 of the OECD Model, together with the U.S. observation set forth in paragraph 15, sets forth a similar understanding of the scope of Article 9 in the context of thin capitalization.

Paragraph 2

When a Contracting State has made an adjustment that is consistent with the provisions of paragraph 1, and the other Contracting State agrees that the adjustment was appropriate to reflect arm's-length conditions, that other Contracting State is obligated to make a correlative adjustment (sometimes referred to as a "corresponding adjustment") to the tax liability of the related person in that other Contracting State. Although the OECD Model does not specify that the other Contracting State must agree with the initial adjustment before it is obligated to make the correlative adjustment, the Commentary makes clear that the paragraph is to be read that way.

As explained in the Commentary to Article 9 of the OECD Model, Article 9 leaves the treatment of "secondary adjustments" to the laws of the Contracting States. When an adjustment under Article 9 has been made, one of the parties will have in its possession funds that it would not have had at arm's length. The question arises as to how to treat these funds. In the United States the general practice is to treat such funds as a dividend or contribution to capital, depending on the relationship between the parties. Under certain circumstances, the parties may be permitted to restore the funds to the party that would have the funds had the transactions been entered into on arm's length terms, and to establish an account payable pending restoration of the funds. See Rev. Proc. 99-32, 1999-2 C.B. 296.

The Contracting State making a secondary adjustment will take the other provisions of the Convention, where relevant, into account. For example, if the effect of a secondary adjustment is to treat a U.S. corporation as having made a distribution of profits to its parent corporation in the other Contracting State, the provisions of Article 10 (Dividends) will apply, and the United States may impose a 5 percent withholding tax on the dividend. Also, if under Article 22 (Relief from Double Taxation) the other State generally gives a credit for taxes paid with respect to such dividends, it would also be required to do so in this case.

The competent authorities are authorized by paragraph 3 of Article 24 (Mutual Agreement Procedure) to consult, if necessary, to resolve any differences in the application of these provisions. For example, there may be a disagreement over whether an adjustment made by a Contracting State under paragraph 1 was appropriate.

If a correlative adjustment is made under paragraph 2, it is to be implemented, pursuant to paragraph 2 of Article 24, notwithstanding any time limits or other procedural limitations in the law of the Contracting State making the adjustment. If a taxpayer has entered a closing agreement (or other written settlement) with the United States prior to bringing a case to the competent authorities, the U.S. competent authority will endeavor only to obtain a correlative adjustment from Iceland. See, Rev. Proc. 2006-54, 2006-49 I.R.B.1035, Section 7.05.

Relationship to Other Articles

The saving clause of paragraph 4 of Article 1 (General Scope) does not apply to paragraph 2 of Article 9 by virtue of an exception to the saving clause in subparagraph 5(a) of Article 1. Thus, even if the statute of limitations has run, a refund of tax can be made in order to implement a correlative adjustment. Statutory or procedural limitations, however, cannot be overridden to impose additional tax, because paragraph 2 of Article 1 provides that the Convention cannot restrict any statutory benefit.

ARTICLE 10 (DIVIDENDS)

Article 10 provides rules for the taxation of dividends paid by a company that is a resident of one Contracting State to a beneficial owner that is a resident of the other Contracting State. The Article provides for full residence State taxation of such dividends and a limited source-State right to tax. Article 10 also provides rules for the imposition of a tax on branch profits by the State of source. Finally, the article prohibits a State from imposing taxes on a company resident in the other Contracting State, other than a branch profits tax, on undistributed earnings.

Paragraph 1

The right of a shareholder's country of residence to tax dividends arising in the source country is preserved by paragraph 1, which permits a Contracting State to tax its residents on dividends paid to them by a company that is a resident of the other Contracting State. For dividends from any other source paid to a resident, Article 20 (Other Income) grants the residence country exclusive taxing jurisdiction (other than for dividends attributable to a permanent establishment in the other State).

Paragraph 2

The State of source also may tax dividends beneficially owned by a resident of the other State, subject to the limitations of paragraphs 2 and 3. Paragraph 2 generally limits the rate of withholding tax in the State of source on dividends paid by a company resident in that State to 15 percent of the gross amount of the dividend. If, however, the beneficial owner of the dividend is a company resident in the other State and owns directly shares representing at least 10 percent of the share capital, as represented as voting power of the company paying the dividend, then the rate of withholding tax in the State of source is limited to 5 percent of the gross amount of the dividend. Shares are considered voting shares if they provide the power to elect, appoint or replace any person vested with the powers ordinarily exercised by the board of directors of a U.S. corporation.

The benefits of paragraph 2 may be granted at the time of payment by means of reduced rate of withholding tax at source. It also is consistent with the paragraph for tax to be withheld at the time of payment at full statutory rates, and the treaty benefit to be granted by means of a subsequent refund so long as such procedures are applied in a reasonable manner.

The determination of whether the ownership threshold for subparagraph 2(a) is met for purposes of the 5 percent maximum rate of withholding tax is made on the date on which entitlement to the dividend is determined. Thus, in the case of a dividend from a U.S. company, the determination of whether the ownership threshold is met generally would be made on the dividend record date.

Paragraph 2 does not affect the taxation of the profits out of which the dividends are paid. The taxation by a Contracting State of the income of its resident companies is governed by the internal law of the Contracting State, subject to the provisions of paragraph 4 of Article 23 (Non-Discrimination).

The term "beneficial owner" is not defined in the Convention, and is, therefore, defined as under the internal law of the country imposing tax (*i.e.*, the source country). The beneficial owner of the dividend for purposes of Article 10 is the person to which the dividend income is attributable for tax purposes under the laws of the source State. Thus, if a dividend paid by a corporation that is a resident of one of the States (as determined under Article 4 (Resident)) is received by a nominee or agent that is a resident of the other State on behalf of a person that is not a resident of that other State, the dividend is not entitled to the benefits of this Article. However, a dividend received by a nominee on behalf of a resident of that other State would be entitled to benefits. These limitations are confirmed by paragraph 12 of the Commentary to Article 10 of the OECD Model.

Special rules, however, apply to shares that are held through fiscally transparent entities. In that case, the rules of paragraph 6 of Article 1 (General Scope) will apply to determine whether the dividends should be treated as having been derived by a resident of a Contracting State. Residence State principles shall be used to determine who derives the dividend, to assure that the dividends for which the source State grants benefits of the Convention will be taken into account for tax purposes by a resident of the residence State. Source State principles of beneficial ownership shall then apply to determine whether the person who derives the dividends, or another resident of the other Contracting State, is the beneficial owner of the dividend. The source State may conclude that the person who derives the dividend in the residence State is a mere nominee, agent, conduit, etc., for a third country resident and deny benefits of the Convention. If the person who derives the dividend under paragraph 6 of Article 1 would not be treated under the source State's principles for determining beneficial ownership as a nominee, agent, custodian, conduit, etc., that person will be treated as the beneficial owner of the income, profits or gains for purposes of the Convention.

Assume, for instance, that a company resident in Iceland pays a dividend to LLC, an entity which is treated as fiscally transparent for U.S. tax purposes but is treated as a company for Icelandic tax purposes. USCo, a company incorporated in the United States, is the sole interest holder in LLC. Paragraph 6 of Article 1 provides that USCo derives the dividend. Iceland's principles of beneficial ownership shall then be applied to USCo. If under the laws of Iceland USCo is found not to be the beneficial owner of the dividend, USCo will not be entitled to the benefits of Article 10 with respect to such dividend. The payment may be entitled to benefits, however, if USCo is found to be a nominee, agent, custodian or conduit for a person who is a resident of the United States.

Beyond identifying the person to whom the principles of beneficial ownership shall be applied, the principles of paragraph 6 of Article 1 will also apply when determining whether other requirements, such as the ownership threshold of subparagraph 2(a) have been satisfied.

For example, assume that IceCo, a company that is a resident of Iceland, owns all of the outstanding shares in ThirdDE, an entity that is disregarded for U.S. tax purposes that is resident in a third country. ThirdDE owns 100% of the stock of USCo. Iceland views ThirdDE as fiscally transparent under its domestic law, and taxes IceCo currently on the income derived by ThirdDE. In this case, IceCo is treated as deriving the dividends paid by USCo under paragraph 6 of Article 1. Moreover, IceCo is treated as owning the shares of USCo directly. The Convention does not address what constitutes direct ownership for purposes of Article 10. As a result, whether ownership is direct is determined under the internal law of the country imposing tax (i.e., the source country) unless the context otherwise requires. Accordingly, a company that holds stock through such an entity will generally be considered to directly own such stock for purposes of Article 10.

This result may change, however, if ThirdDE is regarded as non-fiscally transparent under the laws of Iceland. Assuming that ThirdDE is treated as non-fiscally transparent by

29

Iceland, the income will not be treated as derived by a resident of Iceland for purposes of the Convention. However, ThirdDE may still be entitled to the benefits of the U.S. tax treaty, if any, with its country of residence.

The same principles would apply in determining whether companies holding shares through fiscally transparent entities such as partnerships, trusts, and estates would qualify for benefits. As a result, companies holding shares through such entities may be able to claim the benefits of subparagraph 2(a) under certain circumstances. The lower rate applies when the company's proportionate share of the shares held by the intermediate entity meets the 10 percent threshold, and the company meets the requirements of Article 1(6) (i.e., the company's country of residence treats the intermediate entity as fiscally transparent) with respect to the dividend. Whether this ownership threshold is satisfied may be difficult to determine and often will require an analysis of the partnership or trust agreement.

Paragraph 3

Paragraph 3 imposes limitations on the rate reductions provided by paragraphs 2 and 3 in the case of dividends paid by RIC or a REIT.

The first sentence of subparagraph 3(a) provides that dividends paid by a RIC or REIT are not eligible for the 5 percent rate of withholding tax of subparagraph 2(a).

The second sentence of subparagraph 3(a) provides that the 15 percent maximum rate of withholding tax of subparagraph 2(b) applies to dividends paid by RICs.

The third sentence of subparagraph 3(a) provides that the 15 percent rate of withholding tax also applies to dividends paid by a REIT provided that one of the three following conditions is met. First, the beneficial owner of the dividend is an individual or a pension fund, in either case holding an interest of not more than 10 percent in the REIT. Second, the dividend is paid with respect to a class of stock that is publicly traded and the beneficial owner of the dividend is a person holding an interest of not more than 5 percent of any class of the REIT's shares. Third, the beneficial owner of the dividend holds an interest in the REIT of not more than 10 percent and the REIT is "diversified." A REIT is diversified if the gross value of no single interest in real property held by the REIT exceeds 10 percent of the gross value of the REIT's total interest in real property. Foreclosure property is not considered an interest in real property, and a REIT holding a partnership interest is treated as owning its proportionate share of any interest in real property held by the partnership.

The restrictions set out above are intended to prevent the use of these entities to gain inappropriate U.S. tax benefits. For example, a company resident in Iceland that wishes to hold a diversified portfolio of U.S. corporate shares could hold the portfolio directly and would bear a U.S. withholding tax of 15 percent on all of the dividends that it receives. Alternatively, it could hold the same diversified portfolio by purchasing 10 percent or more of the interests in a RIC. If the RIC is a pure conduit, there may be no U.S. tax cost to interposing the RIC in the chain of ownership. Absent the special rule in paragraph 3, such use of the RIC could transform portfolio dividends, taxable in the United States under the Convention at a 15 percent maximum rate of withholding tax, into direct investment dividends taxable at a 5 percent maximum rate of withholding tax or eligible for the elimination of source-country withholding tax on dividends paid to pension funds as provided in paragraph 4.

30

Similarly, a resident of Iceland directly holding U.S. real property would pay U.S. tax upon the sale of the property either at a 30 percent rate of withholding tax on the gross income or at graduated rates on the net income. As in the preceding example, by placing the real property in a REIT, the investor could, absent a special rule, transform income from the sale of real estate into dividend income from the REIT, taxable at the rates provided in Article 10, significantly reducing the U.S. tax that otherwise would be imposed. Paragraph 3 prevents this result and thereby avoids a disparity between the taxation of direct real estate investments and real estate investments made through REIT conduits. In the cases in which paragraph 3 allows a dividend from a REIT to be eligible for the 15 percent rate of withholding tax, the holding in the REIT is not considered the equivalent of a direct holding in the underlying real property.

Paragraph 4

Paragraph 4 provides that dividends beneficially owned by a pension scheme or employee benefits organization may not be taxed in the Contracting State of which the company paying the tax is a resident. However, the exemption provided in paragraph 4 shall not apply if the dividends are derived from the carrying on of a business, directly or indirectly, by the pension scheme or employee benefits organization. For these purposes, the term "pension scheme" is defined in subparagraph 1(l) of Article 3 (General Definitions).

The exemption is provided because pension schemes and employee benefits organizations normally do not pay tax (either through a general exemption or because reserves for future pension liabilities effectively offset all of the fund's income), and therefore cannot benefit from a foreign tax credit. Moreover, distributions from a pension fund generally do not maintain the character of the underlying income, so the beneficiaries of the pension are not in a position to claim a foreign tax credit when they finally receive the pension, in many cases years after the withholding tax has been paid. Accordingly, in the absence of this rule, the dividends would almost certainly be subject to unrelieved double taxation.

Paragraph 5

Paragraph 5 defines the term dividends broadly and flexibly. The definition is intended to cover all arrangements that yield a return on an equity investment in a corporation as determined under the tax law of the state of source, as well as arrangements that might be developed in the future.

The term includes income from shares, or other corporate rights that are not treated as debt under the law of the source State, that participate in the profits of the company. The term also includes income that is subjected to the same tax treatment as income from shares by the law of the State of source. Thus, a constructive dividend that results from a non-arm's length transaction between a corporation and a related party is a dividend. In the case of the United States the term dividend includes amounts treated as a dividend under U.S. law upon the sale or redemption of shares or upon a transfer of shares in a reorganization. See, e.g., Rev. Rul. 92-85, 1992-2 C.B. 69 (sale of foreign subsidiary=s stock to U.S. sister company is a deemed dividend to extent of the subsidiary's and sister company's earnings and profits). Further, a distribution from a U.S. publicly traded limited partnership, which is taxed as a corporation under U.S. law, is a dividend for purposes of Article 10. However, a distribution by a limited liability company is not taxable by the United States under Article 10, provided the limited liability company is not characterized as an association taxable as a corporation under U.S. law.

Finally, a payment denominated as interest that is made by a thinly capitalized corporation may be treated as a dividend to the extent that the debt is recharacterized as equity under the laws of the source State.

Paragraph 6

Paragraph 6 provides a rule for taxing dividends paid with respect to holdings that form part of the business property of a permanent establishment. In such case, the rules of Article 7 (Business Profits) shall apply. Accordingly, the dividends will be taxed on a net basis using the rates and rules of taxation generally applicable to residents of the State in which the permanent establishment is located, as such rules may be modified by the Convention. An example of dividends paid with respect to the business property of a permanent establishment would be dividends derived by a dealer in stock or securities from stock or securities that the dealer held for sale to customers.

Paragraph 7

The right of a Contracting State to tax dividends paid by a company that is a resident of the other Contracting State is restricted by paragraph 7 to cases in which the dividends are paid to a resident of that Contracting State or are attributable to a permanent establishment or fixed base in that Contracting State. Thus, a Contracting State may not impose a "secondary" withholding tax on dividends paid by a nonresident company out of earnings and profits from that Contracting State

The paragraph also restricts the right of a Contracting State to impose corporate level taxes on undistributed profits, other than a branch profits tax. The paragraph does not restrict a State's right to tax its resident shareholders on undistributed earnings of a corporation resident in the other State. Thus, the authority of the United States to impose taxes on subpart F income and on earnings deemed invested in U.S. property, and its tax on income of a passive foreign investment company that is a qualified electing fund is in no way restricted by this provision.

Paragraph 8

Paragraph 8 permits a Contracting State to impose a branch profits tax on a company resident in the other Contracting State. The tax is in addition to other taxes permitted by the Convention. The term "company" is defined in subparagraph 1(d) of Article 3 (General Definitions).

A Contracting State may impose a branch profits tax on a company if the company has income attributable to a permanent establishment in that Contracting State, derives income from real property in that Contracting State that is taxed on a net basis under Article 6 (Income from Immovable Property (Real Property)), or realizes gains taxable in that State under paragraph 1 of Article 13 (Capital Gains). In the case of the United States, the imposition of such tax is limited, however, to the portion of the aforementioned items of income that represents the amount of such income that is the "dividend equivalent amount." This is consistent with the relevant rules under the U.S. branch profits tax, and the term dividend equivalent amount is defined in paragraph 4 of the Protocol as that portion of the income mentioned in paragraph 7 of Article 10 that is comparable to the amount that would be distributed as a dividend if such income were earned by a subsidiary incorporated in the United States. For any year, a foreign corporation's dividend equivalent amount is equal to the after-tax earnings attributable to the foreign corporation's (i) income attributable to a permanent establishment in the United States, (ii) income from real property in the United States that is taxed on a net basis under Article 6 (Income from Immovable Property (Real Property)), and (iii) gain from a real property interest taxable by the United States under paragraph 1 of Article 13 (Capital Gains), reduced by any increase in the foreign corporation's net investment in U.S. assets or increased by any reduction in the foreign corporation's net investment in U.S. assets.

The dividend equivalent amount for any year approximates the dividend that a U.S. branch office would have paid during the year if the branch had been operated as a separate U.S. subsidiary company. If Iceland also imposes a branch profits tax, the base of its tax must be limited to an amount that is analogous to the dividend equivalent amount.

As discussed in the Technical Explanations to Articles 1(2) and 7(2), consistency principles require that a taxpayer may not mix and match the rules of the Code and the Convention in an inconsistent manner. In the context of the branch profits tax, the consistency requirement means that an enterprise that uses the principles of Article 7 to determine its net taxable income also must use the principles in determining the dividend equivalent amount. Similarly, an enterprise that uses U.S. domestic law to determine its net taxable income must also use U.S. domestic law in complying with the branch profits tax. As in the case of Article 7, if an enterprise switches between domestic law and treaty principles from year to year, it will need to make appropriate adjustments or recapture amounts that otherwise might go untaxed.

Paragraph 9

Paragraph 9 provides that the branch profits tax shall not be imposed at a rate exceeding the direct investment dividend withholding rate of five percent.

Relationship to Other Articles

Notwithstanding the foregoing limitations on source country taxation of dividends, the saving clause of paragraph 4 of Article 1 permits the United States to tax dividends received by its residents and citizens, subject to the special foreign tax credit rules of paragraph 4 of Article 22 (Relief from Double Taxation), as if the Convention had not come into effect.

The benefits of this Article are also subject to the provisions of Article 21 (Limitation on Benefits). Thus, if a resident of the other Contracting State is the beneficial owner of dividends paid by a U.S. corporation, the shareholder must qualify for treaty benefits under at least one of the tests of Article 21 in order to receive the benefits of this Article.

ARTICLE 11 (INTEREST)

Article 11 specifies the taxing jurisdictions over interest income of the States of source and residence and defines the terms necessary to apply the Article.

Paragraph 1

Paragraph 1 generally grants to the State of residence the exclusive right to tax interest beneficially owned by its residents and arising in the other Contracting State.

The term "beneficial owner" is not defined in the Convention, and is, therefore, defined under the internal law of the State of source. The beneficial owner of the interest for purposes of

Article 11 is the person to which the income is attributable under the laws of the source State. Thus, if interest arising in a Contracting State is received by a nominee or agent that is a resident of the other State on behalf of a person that is not a resident of that other State, the interest is not entitled to the benefits of Article 11. However, interest received by a nominee on behalf of a resident of that other State would be entitled to benefits. These limitations are confirmed by paragraph 9 of the OECD Commentary to Article 11.

Paragraph 2

The term "interest" as used in Article 11 is defined in paragraph 2 to include, *inter alia*, income from debt claims of every kind, whether or not secured by a mortgage. Penalty charges for late payment are excluded from the definition of interest. Interest that is paid or accrued subject to a contingency is within the ambit of Article 11. This includes income from a debt obligation carrying the right to participate in profits. The term does not, however, include amounts that are treated as dividends under Article 10 (Dividends).

The term interest also includes amounts subject to the same tax treatment as income from money lent under the law of the State in which the income arises. Thus, for purposes of the Convention, amounts that the United States will treat as interest include (i) the difference between the issue price and the stated redemption price at maturity of a debt instrument (*i.e.*, original issue discount ("OID")), which may be wholly or partially realized on the disposition of a debt instrument (section 1273), (ii) amounts that are imputed interest on a deferred sales contract (section 483), (iii) amounts treated as interest or OID under the stripped bond rules (section 1286), (iv) amounts treated as original issue discount under the below-market interest rate rules (section 7872), (v) a partner's distributive share of a partnership's interest income (section 702), (vi) the interest portion of periodic payments made under a "finance lease" or similar contractual arrangement that in substance is a borrowing by the nominal lessee to finance the acquisition of property, (vii) amounts included in the income of a holder of a residual interest in a REMIC (section 860E), because these amounts generally are subject to the same taxation treatment as interest under U.S. tax law, and (viii) interest with respect to notional principal contracts that are re-characterized as loans because of a "substantial non-periodic payment."

Paragraph 3

Paragraph 3 provides an exception to the exclusive residence taxation rule of paragraph 1 and the source-country gross taxation rule of paragraph 5 in cases where the beneficial owner of the interest carries on business through a permanent establishment in the State of source situated in that State and the interest is attributable to that permanent establishment. In such cases the provisions of Article 7 (Business Profits) will apply and the State of source will retain the right to impose tax on such interest income.

In the case of a permanent establishment that once existed in the State but that no longer exists, the provisions of paragraph 3 also apply, by virtue of paragraph 7 of Article 7, to interest that would be attributable to such a permanent establishment or fixed base if it did exist in the year of payment or accrual. See the Technical Explanation of paragraph 7 of Article 7.

Paragraph 4

Paragraph 4 provides that in cases involving special relationships between the payor and the beneficial owner of interest income, Article 11 applies only to that portion of the total interest payments that would have been made absent such special relationships (*i.e.*, an arm's-length interest payment). Any excess amount of interest paid remains taxable according to the laws of the United States and Iceland, respectively, with due regard to the other provisions of the Convention. Thus, if the excess amount would be treated under the source country's law as a distribution of profits by a corporation, such amount could be taxed as a dividend rather than as interest, but the tax would be subject, if appropriate, to the rate limitations of paragraph 2 of Article 10.

The term "special relationship" is not defined in the Convention. In applying this paragraph the United States considers the term to include the relationships described in Article 9, which in turn corresponds to the definition of "control" for purposes of section 482 of the Code.

This paragraph does not address cases where, owing to a special relationship between the payer and the beneficial owner or between both of them and some other person, the amount of the interest is less than an arm's-length amount. In those cases a transaction may be characterized to reflect its substance and interest may be imputed consistent with the definition of interest in paragraph 3. The United States would apply section 482 or 7872 of the Code to determine the amount of imputed interest in those cases.

Paragraph 5

Paragraph 5 provides anti-abuse exceptions to the source-country exemption in paragraph 1 for two classes of interest payments.

The first class of interest, dealt with in subparagraph 5(a) is so-called "contingent interest." Under this provision, interest arising in a Contracting State that is determined by reference to the receipts, sales, income, profits or other cash flow of the debtor or a related person, to any change in the value of any property of the debtor or a related person or to any dividend, partnership distribution or similar payment made by the debtor or a related person, and paid to a resident of the other State may also be taxed in the Contracting State. Any such interest may be taxed in that Contracting State according to the laws of that State. However, if the beneficial owner is a resident of the other Contracting State, the gross amount of the interest may be taxed at a rate not exceeding 15 percent.

The second class of interest is dealt with in subparagraph 5(b). This exception is consistent with the policy of Code sections 860E(e) and 860G(b) that excess inclusions with respect to a real estate mortgage investment conduit (REMIC) should bear full U.S. tax in all cases. Without a full tax at source foreign purchasers of residual interests would have a competitive advantage over U.S. purchasers at the time these interests are initially offered. Also, absent this rule, the U.S. fisc would suffer a revenue loss with respect to mortgages held in a REMIC because of opportunities for tax avoidance created by differences in the timing of taxable and economic income produced by these interests.

Relationship to Other Articles

Notwithstanding the foregoing limitations on source country taxation of interest, the saving clause of paragraph 4 of Article 1 (General Scope) permits the United States to tax its residents and citizens, subject to the special foreign tax credit rules of paragraph 4 of Article 22 (Relief from Double Taxation), as if the Convention had not come into force.

As with other benefits of the Convention, the benefits of Article 11 are available to a resident of the other State only if that resident is entitled to those benefits under the provisions of Article 21 (Limitation on Benefits).

ARTICLE 12 (ROYALTIES)

Article 12 provides rules for the taxation of royalties arising in one Contracting State and paid to a beneficial owner that is a resident of the other Contracting State.

Paragraph 1

Paragraph 1 generally grants to the State of residence the exclusive right to tax royalties beneficially owned by its residents and arising in the other Contracting State.

The term "beneficial owner" is not defined in the Convention, and is, therefore, defined under the internal law of the State of source. The beneficial owner of the royalty for purposes of Article 12 is the person to which the income is attributable under the laws of the source State. Thus, if a royalty arising in a Contracting State is received by a nominee or agent that is a resident of the other State on behalf of a person that is not a resident of that other State, the royalty is not entitled to the benefits of Article 12. However, a royalty received by a nominee on behalf of a resident of that other State would be entitled to benefits. These limitations are confirmed by paragraph 4 of the OECD Commentary to Article 12.

Paragraph 2

Paragraph 2 provides that notwithstanding the provisions of paragraph 1, the following royalties may be taxed in the Contracting State in which they arise: royalties paid in consideration for the use of, or the right to use a trademark and any information concerning industrial, commercial or scientific experience provided in connection with a rental or franchise agreement that includes rights to use a trademark, and royalties paid in consideration for the use of or the right to use a motion picture film or work on film or videotape or other means of reproduction for use in connection with television. If, however, the beneficial owner of the royalty is a resident of the other Contracting State, the tax may not exceed 5 percent of the gross amount of the royalties.

Paragraph 3

Paragraph 2 defines the term "royalties," as used in Article 12, to include any consideration for the use of, or the right to use, any copyright of literary, artistic, scientific or other work (such as computer software and cinematographic films), any patent, trademark, design or model, plan, secret formula or process, or for information concerning industrial, commercial, or scientific experience. The term "royalties," however, does not include income from leasing personal property.

The term royalties is defined in the Convention and therefore is generally independent of domestic law. Certain terms used in the definition are not defined in the Convention, but these may be defined under domestic tax law. For example, the term "secret process or formulas" is found in the Code, and its meaning has been elaborated in the context of sections 351 and 367. See Rev. Rul. 55-17, 1955-1 C.B. 388; Rev. Rul. 64-56, 1964-1 C.B. 133; Rev. Proc. 69-19, 1969-2 C.B. 301.

Consideration for the use or right to use cinematographic films, or works on film, tape, or other means of reproduction in radio or television broadcasting is specifically included in the definition of royalties. It is intended that, with respect to any subsequent technological advances in the field of radio or television broadcasting, consideration received for the use of such technology will also be included in the definition of royalties.

If an artist who is resident in one Contracting State records a performance in the other Contracting State, retains a copyrighted interest in a recording, and receives payments for the right to use the recording based on the sale or public playing of the recording, then the right of such other Contracting State to tax those payments is governed by Article 12. See Boulez v. Commissioner, 83 T.C. 584 (1984), aff'd, 810 F.2d 209 (D.C. Cir. 1986). By contrast, if the artist earns in the other Contracting State income covered by Article 16 (Entertainers and Sportsmen), for example, endorsement income from the artist's attendance at a film screening, and if such income also is attributable to one of the rights described in Article 12 (*e.g.*, the use of the artist's photograph in promoting the screening), Article 16 and not Article 12 is applicable to such income.

Computer software generally is protected by copyright laws around the world. Under the Convention, consideration received for the use, or the right to use, computer software is treated either as royalties or as business profits, depending on the facts and circumstances of the transaction giving rise to the payment.

The primary factor in determining whether consideration received for the use, or the right to use, computer software is treated as royalties or as business profits is the nature of the rights transferred. See Treas. Reg. section 1.861-18. The fact that the transaction is characterized as a license for copyright law purposes is not dispositive. For example, a typical retail sale of "shrink wrap" software generally will not be considered to give rise to royalty income, even though for copyright law purposes it may be characterized as a license.

The means by which the computer software is transferred are not relevant for purposes of the analysis. Consequently, if software is electronically transferred but the rights obtained by the transferee are substantially equivalent to rights in a program copy, the payment will be considered business profits.

The term "industrial, commercial, or scientific experience" (sometimes referred to as "know-how") has the meaning ascribed to it in paragraph 11 *et seq.* of the Commentary to Article 12 of the OECD Model. Consistent with that meaning, the term may include information that is ancillary to a right otherwise giving rise to royalties, such as a patent or secret process.

Know-how also may include, in limited cases, technical information that is conveyed through technical or consultancy services. It does not include general educational training of the user's employees, nor does it include information developed especially for the user, such as a technical plan or design developed according to the user's specifications. Thus, as provided in paragraph 11.3 of the Commentary to Article 12 of the OECD Model, the term "royalties" does not include payments received as consideration for after-sales service, for services rendered by a seller to a purchaser under a warranty, or for pure technical assistance.

The term "royalties" also does not include payments for professional services (such as architectural, engineering, legal, managerial, medical, software development services). For example, income from the design of a refinery by an engineer (even if the engineer employed know-how in the process of rendering the design) or the production of a legal brief by a lawyer is not income from the transfer of know-how taxable under Article 12, but is income from services taxable under either Article 7 (Business Profits) or Article 14 (Income from Employment). Professional services may be embodied in property that gives rise to royalties, however. Thus, if a professional contracts to develop patentable property and retains rights in the resulting property under the development contract, subsequent license payments made for those rights would be royalties.

Paragraph 4

This paragraph provides an exception in cases where the beneficial owner of the royalties carries on business through a permanent establishment in the state of source and the royalties are attributable to that permanent establishment. In such cases the provisions of Article 7 will apply.

The provisions of paragraph 7 of Article 7 apply to this paragraph. For example, royalty income that is attributable to a permanent establishment and that accrues during the existence of the permanent establishment, but is received after the permanent establishment no longer exists, remains taxable under the provisions of Article 7, and not under this Article.

Paragraph 5

Paragraph 5 contains the source rule for royalties. Under paragraph 5, royalties are treated as arising in a Contracting State if paid by a resident of that State. As an exception, royalties that are attributable to a permanent establishment in a Contracting State and borne by the permanent establishment are considered to arise in that State. Where, however, the payor of the royalties is not a resident of either Contracting State, and the royalties are not borne by a permanent establishment in either Contracting State, but the royalties are for the use of, or the right to use, in one of the Contracting States, any property or right described in paragraph 3, the royalties are deemed to arise in that State.

Paragraph 6

Paragraph 6 provides that in cases involving special relationships between the payor and beneficial owner of royalties, Article 12 applies only to the extent the royalties would have been paid absent such special relationships (i.e., an arm's-length royalty). Any excess amount of royalties paid remains taxable according to the laws of the two Contracting States, with due regard to the other provisions of the Convention. If, for example, the excess amount is treated as a distribution of corporate profits under domestic law, such excess amount will be taxed as a dividend rather than as royalties, but the tax imposed on the dividend payment will be subject to the rate limitations of paragraph 2 of Article 10 (Dividends).

Relationship to Other Articles

Notwithstanding the foregoing limitations on source country taxation of royalties, the saving clause of paragraph 4 of Article 1 (General Scope) permits the United States to tax its residents and citizens, subject to the special foreign tax credit rules of paragraph 4 of Article 22 (Relief from Double Taxation), as if the Convention had not come into force.

As with other benefits of the Convention, the benefits of Article 12 are available to a resident of the other State only if that resident is entitled to those benefits under Article 21 (Limitation on Benefits).

ARTICLE 13 (CAPITAL GAINS)

Article 13 assigns either primary or exclusive taxing jurisdiction over gains from the alienation of property to the State of residence or the State of source.

Paragraph 1

Paragraph 1 of Article 13 preserves the non-exclusive right of the State of source to tax from the alienation of immovable property (real property) situated in that State. For purposes of paragraph 1, in all events the term "immovable property (real property) situated in the other State" includes a United States real property interest in the United States, as that term is defined in the Internal Revenue Code on the date of signature of the Convention, and as amended (without changing the general principles of paragraph 1). Thus, the United States preserves its right to collect the tax imposed by section 897 of the Code on gains derived by foreign persons from the disposition of United States real property interests, including gains arising from indirect dispositions described in section 897(h).

Paragraph 2

This paragraph defines the term "immovable property (real property) situated in the other Contracting State." The term includes real property referred to in Article 6 (i.e., an interest in the real property itself), rights to assets to be produced by the exploration or exploitation of the seabed and subsoil of that other State and their natural resources, including rights to interests in or the benefit of such assets, a "United States real property interest" (when the United States is the other Contracting State under paragraph 1), and, as specified in subparagraph 2(d), an equivalent interest in immovable property (real property) situated in Iceland.

Under section 897(c) of the Code the term "United States real property interest" includes shares in a U.S. corporation that owns sufficient U.S. real property interests to satisfy an asset-ratio test on certain testing dates. The term also includes certain foreign corporations that have elected to be treated as U.S. corporations for this purpose. Section 897(i).

Paragraph 3

Paragraph 3 of Article 13 deals with the taxation of certain gains from the alienation of movable property forming part of the business property of a permanent establishment that an enterprise of a Contracting State has in the other Contracting State. This also includes gains from the alienation of such a permanent establishment (alone or with the whole enterprise). Such gains may be taxed in the State in which the permanent establishment is located.

A resident of Iceland that is a partner in a partnership doing business in the United States generally will have a permanent establishment in the United States as a result of the activities of the partnership, assuming that the activities of the partnership rise to the level of a permanent establishment. Rev. Rul. 91-32, 1991-1 C.B. 107. Further, under paragraph 3, the United States generally may tax a partner's distributive share of income realized by a partnership on the disposition of movable property forming part of the business property of the partnership in the United States.

The gains subject to paragraph 3 may be taxed in the State in which the permanent establishment is located, regardless of whether the permanent establishment exists at the time of the alienation. This rule incorporates the rule of section 864(c)(6) of the Code. Accordingly, income that is attributable to a permanent establishment, but that is deferred and received after the permanent establishment no longer exists, may nevertheless be taxed by the State in which the permanent establishment was located.

Paragraph 4

This paragraph limits the taxing jurisdiction of the State of source with respect to gains from the alienation of ships, aircraft or containers operated in international traffic by the enterprise alienating the ship or aircraft and from property (other than real property) pertaining to the operation or use of such ships, aircraft, or containers.

Under paragraph 4, such income is taxable only in the Contracting State in which the alienator is resident. Notwithstanding paragraph 3, the rules of this paragraph apply even if the income is attributable to a permanent establishment maintained by the enterprise in the other Contracting State. This result is consistent with the allocation of taxing rights under Article 8 (Shipping and Air Transport).

Paragraph 5

Paragraph 5 grants to the State of residence of the alienator the exclusive right to tax gains from the alienation of property other than property referred to in paragraphs 1 through 4. For example, gain derived from shares, other than shares described in paragraphs 2 or 3, debt instruments and various financial instruments, may be taxed only in the State of residence, to the extent such income is not otherwise characterized as income taxable under another article (e.g., Article 10 (Dividends) or Article 11 (Interest)). Similarly gain derived from the alienation of tangible personal property, other than tangible personal property described in paragraph 3, may be taxed only in the State of residence of the alienator.

Gains derived by a resident of a Contracting State from real property located in a third state are not taxable in the other Contracting State, even if the sale is attributable to a permanent establishment located in the other Contracting State.

Paragraph 6

Paragraph 6 sets forth a rule which permits the imposition of certain expatriation taxes. This rule provides that notwithstanding paragraph 5 a Contracting State may tax gains from the alienation of shares or rights in a company, the capital of which is wholly or partly divided into shares, and that is a resident of that State, if the person alienating the shares or rights is an individual resident in the other Contracting State, but only if such individual was a resident of the first-mentioned State at any time during the five-year period preceding the alienation.

Relationship to Other Articles

Notwithstanding the foregoing limitations on taxation of certain gains by the State of source, the saving clause of paragraph 4 of Article 1 (General Scope) permits the United States to tax its citizens and residents as if the Convention had not come into effect. Thus, any limitation in this Article on the right of the United States to tax gains does not apply to gains of a U.S. citizen or resident.

The benefits of this Article are also subject to the provisions of Article 21 (Limitation on Benefits). Thus, only a resident of a Contracting State that satisfies one of the conditions in Article 21 is entitled to the benefits of this Article.

Additionally, the provisions of paragraph 6 shall be applied in conjunction with subparagraph 2(b) of Article 22 (Relief from Double Taxation).

ARTICLE 14 (INCOME FROM EMPLOYMENT)

Article 14 apportions taxing jurisdiction over remuneration derived by a resident of a Contracting State as an employee between the States of source and residence.

Paragraph 1

The general rule of Article 14 is contained in paragraph 1. Remuneration derived by a resident of a Contracting State as an employee may be taxed by the State of residence, and the remuneration also may be taxed by the other Contracting State to the extent derived from employment exercised (*i.e.*, services performed) in that other Contracting State. Paragraph 1 also provides that the more specific rules of Articles 15 (Directors' Fees), 17 (Pensions, Social Security, and Annuities), and 19 (Government Service) apply in the case of employment income described in one of those articles. Thus, even though the State of source has a right to tax employment income under Article 14, it may not have the right to tax that income under the Convention if the income is described, for example, in Article 17 (Pensions, Social Security, and Annuities) and is not taxable in the State of source under the provisions of that article.

Article 14 applies to any form of compensation for employment, including payments in kind. Paragraph 1.1 of the Commentary to Article 16 of the OECD Model now confirms that interpretation.

Consistent with section 864(c)(6) of the Code, Article 14 also applies regardless of the timing of actual payment for services. Consequently, a person who receives the right to a future payment in consideration for services rendered in a Contracting State would be taxable in that State even if the payment is received at a time when the recipient is a resident of the other Contracting State. Thus, a bonus paid to a resident of a Contracting State with respect to services performed in the other Contracting State with respect to a particular taxable year would be subject to Article 14 for that year even if it was paid after the close of the year. An annuity received for services performed in a taxable year could be subject to Article 14 despite the fact that it was paid in subsequent years. In that case, it would be necessary to determine whether the payment constitutes deferred compensation, taxable under Article 14, or a qualified pension subject to the rules of Article 17 (Pensions, Social Security, and Annuities). Article 14 also applies to income derived from the exercise of stock options granted with respect to services performed in the host State, even if those stock options are exercised after the employee has left the source country. If Article 14 is found to apply, whether such payments were taxable in the State where the employment was exercised would depend on whether the tests of paragraph 2 were satisfied in the year in which the services to which the payment relates were performed.

Paragraph 2

Paragraph 2 sets forth an exception to the general rule that employment income may be taxed in the State where it is exercised. Under paragraph 2, the State where the employment is exercised may not tax the income from the employment if three conditions are satisfied: (a) the individual is present in the other Contracting State for a period or periods not exceeding 183 days in any 12-month period that begins or ends during the relevant taxable year (i.e., in the United States, the calendar year in which the services are performed); (b) the remuneration is paid by, or on behalf of, an employer who is not a resident of that other Contracting State; and (c) the remuneration is not borne as a deductible expense by a permanent establishment that the employer has in that other State. In order for the remuneration to be exempt from tax in the source State, all three conditions must be satisfied. This exception is identical to that set forth in the OECD Model.

The 183-day period in condition (a) is to be measured using the "days of physical presence" method. Under this method, the days that are counted include any day in which a part of the day is spent in the host country. (Rev. Rul. 56-24, 1956-1 C.B. 851.) Thus, days that are counted include the days of arrival and departure; weekends and holidays on which the employee does not work but is present within the country; vacation days spent in the country before, during or after the employment period, unless the individual's presence before or after the employment can be shown to be independent of his presence there for employment purposes; and time during periods of sickness, training periods, strikes, etc., when the individual is present but not working. If illness prevented the individual from leaving the country in sufficient time to qualify for the benefit, those days will not count. Also, any part of a day spent in the host country while in transit between two points outside the host country is not counted. If the individual is a resident of the host country for part of the taxable year concerned and a nonresident for the remainder of the year, the individual's days of presence as a resident do not count for purposes of determining whether the 183-day period is exceeded.

Conditions (b) and (c) are intended to ensure that a Contracting State will not be required to allow a deduction to the payor for compensation paid and at the same time to exempt the employee on the amount received. Accordingly, if a foreign person pays the salary of an employee who is employed in the host State, but a host State corporation or permanent establishment reimburses the payor with a payment that can be identified as a reimbursement, neither condition (b) nor (c), as the case may be, will be considered to have been fulfilled.

The reference to remuneration "borne by" a permanent establishment is understood to encompass all expenses that economically are incurred and not merely expenses that are currently deductible for tax purposes. Accordingly, the expenses referred to include expenses that are capitalizable as well as those that are currently deductible. Further, salaries paid by residents that are exempt from income taxation may be considered to be borne by a permanent establishment notwithstanding the fact that the expenses will be neither deductible nor capitalizable since the payor is exempt from tax.
Paragraph 3

Paragraph 3 contains a special rule applicable to remuneration for services performed by a resident of a Contracting State as an employee aboard a ship or aircraft operated in international traffic. Such remuneration may be taxed only in the State of residence of the employee if the services are performed as a member of the regular complement of the ship or aircraft. The "regular complement" includes the crew. In the case of a cruise ship, for example, it may also include others, such as entertainers, lecturers, etc., employed by the shipping company to serve on the ship throughout its voyage. The use of the term "regular complement" is intended to clarify that a person who exercises his employment as, for example, an insurance salesman while aboard a ship or aircraft is not covered by this paragraph.

If a U.S. citizen who is resident in Iceland performs services as an employee in the United States and meets the conditions of paragraph 2 for source country exemption, he nevertheless is taxable in the United States by virtue of the saving clause of paragraph 4 of Article 1 (General Scope), subject to the special foreign tax credit rule of paragraph 4 of Article 22 (Relief from Double Taxation).

ARTICLE 15 (DIRECTORS' FEES)

This Article provides that a Contracting State may tax the fees and other compensation paid by a company that is a resident of that State for services performed by a resident of the other Contracting State in his capacity as a director of the company. This rule is an exception to the more general rules of Articles 7 (Business Profits) and 14 (Income from Employment). Thus, for example, in determining whether a director's fee paid to a non-employee director is subject to tax in the country of residence of the corporation, it is not relevant to establish whether the fee is attributable to a permanent establishment in that State.

Under this Article, a resident of one Contracting State who is a director of a corporation that is resident in the other Contracting State is subject to tax in that other State in respect of his directors' fees regardless of where the services are performed. Under U.S. law, however, services performed by a nonresident may not be taxed unless they are performed in the United States (unless that nonresident is a U.S. citizen, and therefore subject to the saving clause of paragraph 4 of Article 1 (General Scope)).

ARTICLE 16 (ENTERTAINERS AND SPORTSMEN)

This Article deals with the taxation in a Contracting State of entertainers and sportsmen resident in the other Contracting State from the performance of their services as such. The Article applies both to the income of an entertainer or sportsman who performs services on his own behalf and one who performs services on behalf of another person, either as an employee of that person, or pursuant to any other arrangement. The rules of this Article take precedence, in some circumstances, over those of Articles 7 (Business Profits) and 14 (Income from Employment).

This Article applies only with respect to the income of entertainers and sportsmen. Others involved in a performance or athletic event, such as producers, directors, technicians, managers, coaches, etc., remain subject to the provisions of Articles 7 and 14. In addition, except as provided in paragraph 2, income earned by juridical persons is not covered by Article 16.

Paragraph 1

Paragraph 1 describes the circumstances in which a Contracting State may tax the performance income of an entertainer or sportsman who is a resident of the other Contracting State. Under the paragraph, income derived by an individual resident of a Contracting State from activities as an entertainer or sportsman exercised in the other Contracting State may be taxed in that other State if the amount of the gross receipts derived by the performer exceeds $20,000 (or its equivalent in Icelandic kronur) for the taxable year. The $20,000 includes expenses reimbursed to the individual or borne on his behalf. If the gross receipts exceed $20,000, the full amount, not just the excess, may be taxed in the State of performance.

The Convention introduces the monetary threshold to distinguish between two groups of entertainers and athletes -- those who are paid relatively large sums of money for very short periods of service, and who would, therefore, normally be exempt from host country tax under the standard personal services income rules, and those who earn relatively modest amounts and are, therefore, not easily distinguishable from those who earn other types of personal service income.

Tax may be imposed under paragraph 1 even if the performer would have been exempt from tax under Article 7 or 14. On the other hand. if the performer would be exempt from host-country tax under Article 16, but would be taxable under either Article 7 or 14, tax may be imposed under either of those Articles. Thus, for example, if a performer derives remuneration from his activities in an independent capacity, and the performer does not have a permanent establishment in the host State, he may be taxed by the host State in accordance with Article 16 if his remuneration exceeds $20,000 annually, despite the fact that he generally would be exempt from host State taxation under Article 7. However, a performer who receives less than the $20,000 threshold amount and therefore is not taxable under Article 16 nevertheless may be subject to tax in the host country under Article 7 or 14 if the tests for host-country taxability under the relevant Article are met. For example, if an entertainer who is an independent contractor earns $14,000 of income in a State for the calendar year, but the income is attributable to his permanent establishment in the State of performance, that State may tax his income under Article 7.

Nothing shall preclude a Contracting State from withholding tax from such payments according to its domestic laws. However, if according to the provisions of this Article, such remuneration or income may only be taxed in the other Contracting State, the first-mentioned Contracting State shall make a refund of the tax so withheld upon a duly filed claim. Such claim must be filed with the tax authorities that have collected the withholding tax within five years after the close of the calendar year in which the tax was withheld.

As explained in paragraph 9 of the Commentary to Article 17 of the OECD Model, Article 16 of the Convention applies to all income connected with a performance by the entertainer, such as appearance fees, award or prize money, and a share of the gate receipts. Income derived from a Contracting State by a performer who is a resident of the other Contracting State from other than actual performance, such as royalties from record sales and payments for product endorsements, is not covered by this Article, but by other articles of the Convention, such as Article 12 (Royalties) or Article 7. For example, if an entertainer receives royalty income from the sale of live recordings, the royalty income would be subject to the provisions of Article 12, even if the performance was conducted in the source country, although the entertainer could be taxed in the source country with respect to income from the performance itself under Article 16 if the dollar threshold is exceeded.

In determining whether income falls under Article 16 or another article, the controlling factor will be whether the income in question is predominantly attributable to the performance itself or to other activities or property rights. For instance, a fee paid to a performer for endorsement of a performance in which the performer will participate would be considered to be so closely associated with the performance itself that it normally would fall within Article 16. Similarly, a sponsorship fee paid by a business in return for the right to attach its name to the performance would be so closely associated with the performance that it would fall under Article 16 as well. As indicated in paragraph 9 of the Commentary to Article 17 of the OECD Model, however, a cancellation fee would not be considered to fall within Article 16 but would be dealt with under Article 7 or 14.

As indicated in paragraph 4 of the Commentary to Article 17 of the OECD Model, where an individual fulfills a dual role as performer and non-performer (such as a player-coach or an actor-director), but his role in one of the two capacities is negligible, the predominant character of the individual's activities should control the characterization of those activities. In other cases there should be an apportionment between the performance-related compensation and other compensation.

Consistent with Article 14, Article 16 also applies regardless of the timing of actual payment for services. Thus, a bonus paid to a resident of a Contracting State with respect to a performance in the other Contracting State during a particular taxable year would be subject to Article 16 for that year even if it was paid after the close of the year. The determination as to whether the $20,000 threshold has been exceeded is determined separately with respect to each year of payment. Accordingly, if an actor who is a resident of one Contracting State receives residual payments over time with respect to a movie that was filmed in the other Contracting State, the payments do not have to be aggregated from one year to another to determine whether the total payments have finally exceeded $20,000. Otherwise, residual payments received many years later could retroactively subject all earlier payments to tax by the other Contracting State.

Paragraph 2

Paragraph 2 is intended to address the potential for circumvention of the rule in paragraph 1 when a performer's income does not accrue directly to the performer himself, but to another person. Foreign performers frequently perform in the United States as employees of, or under contract with, a company or other person.

The relationship may truly be one of employee and employer, with no circumvention of paragraph 1 either intended or realized. On the other hand, the "employer" may, for example, be a company established and owned by the performer, which is merely acting as the nominal income recipient in respect of the remuneration for the performance (a "star company"). The performer may act as an "employee," receive a modest salary, and arrange to receive the remainder of the income from his performance from the company in another form or at a later time. In such case, absent the provisions of paragraph 2, the income arguably could escape host-country tax because the company earns business profits but has no permanent establishment in that country. The performer may largely or entirely escape host-country tax by receiving only a small salary, perhaps small enough to place him below the dollar threshold in paragraph 1. The performer might arrange to receive further payments in a later year, when he is not subject to host-country tax, perhaps as dividends or liquidating distributions.

Paragraph 2 seeks to prevent this type of abuse while at the same time protecting the taxpayers' rights to the benefits of the Convention when there is a legitimate employee-employer relationship between the performer and the person providing his services. Under paragraph 2, when the income accrues to a person other than the performer, and the performer or related persons participate, directly or indirectly, in the receipts or profits of that other person, the income may be taxed in the Contracting State where the performer's services are exercised, without regard to the provisions of the Convention concerning business profits or income from employment (Article 14). In cases where paragraph 2 is applicable, the income of the "employer" may be subject to tax in the host Contracting State even if it has no permanent establishment in the host country. Taxation under paragraph 2 is on the person providing the services of the performer. This paragraph does not affect the rules of paragraph 1, which apply to the performer himself. The income taxable by virtue of paragraph 2 is reduced to the extent of salary payments to the performer, which fall under paragraph 1.

For purposes of paragraph 2, income is deemed to accrue to another person (*i.e.*, the person providing the services of the performer) if that other person has control over, or the right to receive, gross income in respect of the services of the performer. Direct or indirect participation in the profits of a person may include, but is not limited to, the accrual or receipt of deferred remuneration, bonuses, fees, dividends, partnership income or other income or distributions.

Paragraph 2 does not apply if it is established that neither the performer nor any persons related to the performer participate directly or indirectly in the receipts or profits of the person providing the services of the performer. Assume, for example, that a circus owned by a U.S. corporation performs in the other Contracting State, and promoters of the performance in the other State pay the circus, which, in turn, pays salaries to the circus performers. The circus is determined to have no permanent establishment in that State. Since the circus performers do not participate in the profits of the circus, but merely receive their salaries out of the circus' gross receipts, the circus is protected by Article 7 and its income is not subject to host-country tax. Whether the salaries of the circus performers are subject to host-country tax under this Article depends on whether they exceed the $20,000 threshold in paragraph 1.

Since pursuant to Article 1 (General Scope) the Convention only applies to persons who are residents of one of the Contracting States, income of the star company would not be eligible for benefits of the Convention if the company is not a resident of one of the Contracting States.

Relationship to other Articles

This Article is subject to the provisions of the saving clause of paragraph 4 of Article 1 (General Scope). Thus, if an entertainer or a sportsman who is resident in the other Contracting State is a citizen of the United States, the United States may tax all of his income from performances in the United States without regard to the provisions of this Article, subject, however, to the special foreign tax credit provisions of paragraph 4 of Article 22 (Relief From Double Taxation). In addition, benefits of this Article are subject to the provisions of Article 21 (Limitation On Benefits).

ARTICLE 17 (PENSIONS, SOCIAL SECURITY, AND ANNUITIES)

This Article deals with the taxation of private (i.e., non-government service) pensions, social security benefits, and annuities.

Paragraph 1

Paragraph 1 provides that distributions from pensions and other similar remuneration paid to a resident of a Contracting State in consideration of past employment are taxable only in the State of residence of the beneficiary. The term "pensions and other similar remuneration" includes both periodic and single sum payments.

The phrase "pensions and other similar remuneration" is intended to encompass payments made by qualified private retirement plans. In the United States, the plans encompassed by Paragraph 1 include: qualified plans under section 401(a), individual retirement plans (including individual retirement plans that are part of a simplified employee pension plan that satisfies section 408(k), individual retirement accounts and section 408(p) accounts), section 403(a) qualified annuity plans, and section 403(b) plans. Distributions from section 457 plans may also fall under Paragraph 1 if they are not paid with respect to government services covered by Article 19. In Iceland, the term pension applies to any pension fund or pension plan qualified under the Pension Act or any identical or substantially similar schemes which are created under any law enacted after the signature of the Convention. The competent authorities may agree that distributions from other plans that generally meet similar criteria to those applicable to the listed plans also qualify for the benefits of Paragraph 1.

Pensions in respect of government services covered by Article 18 are not covered by this paragraph. They are covered either by paragraph 2 of this Article, if they are in the form of social security benefits, or by paragraph 2 of Article 18 (Government Service). Thus, Article 18 generally covers section 457(g), 401(a), 403(a), and 403(b) plans established for government employees, including the Thrift Savings Plan (section 7701(j)).

Paragraph 2

The treatment of social security benefits is dealt with in paragraph 2. This paragraph provides that, notwithstanding the provision of paragraph 1 under which private pensions are taxable exclusively in the State of residence of the beneficial owner, payments made by one of the Contracting States under the provisions of its social security or similar legislation to a resident of Iceland or to a citizen of the United States will be taxable only in the Contracting State making the payment. The reference to U.S. citizens is necessary to ensure that a social security payment by Iceland to a U.S. citizen who is not resident in the United States will not be taxable by the United States.

This paragraph applies to social security beneficiaries whether they have contributed to the system as private sector or Government employees. The phrase "similar legislation" is intended to refer to United States tier 1 Railroad Retirement benefits.

Paragraph 3

Under paragraph 3, annuities that are derived and beneficially owned by a resident of a Contracting State are taxable only in that State. An annuity, as the term is used in this paragraph, means a stated sum paid periodically at stated times during a specified number of years, under an obligation to make the payment in return for adequate and full consideration (other than for services rendered). An annuity received in consideration for services rendered would be treated as either deferred compensation that is taxable in accordance with Article 14 (Income from Employment) or a pension that is subject to the rules of paragraph 1.

Paragraph 4

Paragraph 4 provides that, if a resident of a Contracting State participates in a pension fund established in the other Contracting State, the State of residence will not tax the income of the pension fund with respect to that resident until a distribution is made from the pension fund. Thus, for example, if a U.S. citizen contributes to a U.S. qualified plan while working in the United States and then establishes residence in Iceland, paragraph 1 prevents Iceland from taxing currently the plan's earnings and accretions with respect to that individual. When the resident receives a distribution from the pension fund, that distribution may be subject to tax in the State of residence, subject to paragraph 1.

Relationship to other Articles

Paragraphs 1 and 3 of Article 17 are subject to the saving clause of paragraph 4 of Article 1 (General Scope). Thus, a U.S. citizen who is resident in the other Contracting State, and receives either a pension, annuity or alimony payment from the United States, may be subject to U.S. tax on the payment, notwithstanding the rules in those three paragraphs that give the State of residence of the recipient the exclusive taxing right. Paragraphs 2 and 4 are excepted from the saving clause by virtue of subparagraph 5(a) of Article 1. Thus, the United States will not tax U.S. citizens and residents on the income described in those paragraphs even if such amounts otherwise would be subject to tax under U.S. law.

ARTICLE 18 (GOVERNMENT SERVICE)

Paragraph 1

Subparagraphs 1(a) and 1(b) deal with the taxation of government compensation (other than a pension addressed in paragraph 2). Subparagraph 1(a) provides that remuneration paid from the public funds of a Contracting State or its political subdivisions or local authorities to any individual who is rendering services to that State, political subdivision or local authority, which are in the discharge of governmental functions, is exempt from tax by the other State. Under subparagraph 1(b), such payments are, however, taxable exclusively in the other State (i.e., the host State) if the services are rendered in that other State and the individual is a resident of that State who is either a national of that State or a person who did not become resident of that State solely for purposes of rendering the services. The paragraph applies to anyone performing services for a government, whether as a government employee, an independent contractor, or an employee of an independent contractor.

Paragraph 2

Paragraph 2 deals with the taxation of pensions paid by, or out of funds created by, one of the States, or a political subdivision or a local authority thereof, to an individual in respect of services rendered in the discharge of functions of a governmental nature to that State or subdivision or authority. Subparagraph 1(a) provides that such pensions are taxable only in that State. Subparagraph 1(b) provides an exception under which such pensions are taxable only in the other State if the individual is a resident of, and a national of, that other State.

Pensions paid to retired civilian and military employees of a Government of either State are intended to be covered under paragraph 2. When benefits paid by a State in respect of services rendered to that State or a subdivision or authority are in the form of social security benefits, however, those payments are covered by paragraph 2 of Article 17 (Pensions, Social Security, Annuities, Alimony, and Child Support). As a general matter, the result will be the same whether Article 17 or 19 applies, since social security benefits are taxable exclusively by the source country and so are government pensions. The result will differ only when the payment is made to a citizen and resident of the other Contracting State, who is not also a citizen of the paying State. In such a case, social security benefits continue to be taxable at source while government pensions become taxable only in the residence country.

Paragraph 3

Paragraph 3 provides that the remuneration described in paragraph 1 will be subject to the rules of Articles 14 (Income from Employment), 15 (Directors' Fees), 16 (Entertainers and Sportsmen) or 17 if the recipient of the income is employed by a business conducted by a government.

Relationship to other Articles

Under subparagraph 5(b) of Article 1 (General Scope), the saving clause (paragraph 4 of Article 1) does not apply to the benefits conferred by one of the States under Article 18 if the recipient of the benefits is neither a citizen of that State, nor a person who has been admitted for permanent residence there (i.e., in the United States, a "green card" holder). Thus, a resident of a Contracting State who in the course of performing functions of a governmental nature becomes a resident of the other State (but not a permanent resident), would be entitled to the benefits of this Article. Similarly, an individual who receives a pension paid by the Government of Iceland in respect of services rendered to the Government of Iceland shall be taxable on this pension only in Iceland unless the individual is a U.S. citizen or acquires a U.S. green card.

ARTICLE 19 (STUDENTS AND TRAINEES)

This Article provides rules for host-country taxation of visiting students and business trainees. Persons who meet the tests of the Article will be exempt from tax in the State that they are visiting with respect to designated classes of income. Several conditions must be satisfied in order for an individual to be entitled to the benefits of this Article.

Paragraph 1

Paragraph 1 provides that an individual who is a resident of one Contracting State at the time he becomes temporarily present in the other Contracting State and who is temporarily present therein for the primary purpose of studying at a university or other recognized educational institution in that other Contracting State, securing training required to qualify him to practice a profession or professional specialty, or studying or doing research as a recipient of a grant, allowance, or award from a governmental, religious, charitable, scientific, literary, or educational organization, will be exempt from tax by that other Contracting State for a period not exceeding five taxable years from the date of his arrival in that other Contracting State on:

(1) Gifts from abroad for the purpose of his maintenance, education, study, research or training;

(2) The grant, allowance, or award; and

(3) Income from personal services performed in the other Contracting State not in excess of $9,000 or its equivalent in Icelandic kronur for any taxable year.

Paragraph 2

Under paragraph 2, an individual who is a resident of one Contracting State at the time he becomes temporarily present in the other Contracting State and who is temporarily present therein as an employee of, or under contract with, a resident of the first-mentioned Contracting State, for the primary purpose of acquiring technical, professional, or business experience from a person other than that resident of the first-mentioned Contracting State or other than a person related to such resident, or studying at a university or other recognized educational institution in that other Contracting State, will be exempt from tax by that other Contracting State for a period of twelve consecutive months on income from personal services not in excess of $9,000 or its equivalent in Icelandic kronur.

Paragraph 3

Paragraph 3 provides an exemption for residents of one Contracting State who become temporarily present in the other Contracting State for purposes of training, research or study in a program sponsored by the other Contracting State. The exemption is available to an individual who is a resident of one Contracting State at the time he becomes temporarily present in the other Contracting State and who is temporarily present in that other Contracting State for a period not exceeding one year, as a participant in a program sponsored by the other Contracting State, for the primary purpose of training, research, or study. A person meeting these requirements will be exempt from tax by the other Contracting State with respect to his income from personal services in respect of such training, research, or study performed in that other Contracting State in an aggregate amount not in excess of $9,000 or its equivalent in Icelandic kronur.

Relationship to other Articles

The saving clause of paragraph 4 of Article 1 (General Scope) does not apply to this Article with respect to an individual who is neither a citizen of the host State nor an individual who has been admitted for permanent residence there. The saving clause, however, does apply with respect to citizens and permanent residents of the host State. Thus, a U.S. citizen who is a resident of Iceland and who visits the United States as a full-time student at an accredited university will not be exempt from U.S. tax on remittances from abroad that otherwise constitute U.S. taxable income. An individual, however, who is not a U.S. citizen, and who visits the United States as a student and remains long enough to become a resident under U.S. law, but does not become a permanent resident (i.e., does not acquire a green card), will be entitled to the full benefits of the Article.

ARTICLE 20 (OTHER INCOME)

Article 20 generally assigns taxing jurisdiction over income not dealt with in the other articles (Articles 6 (Income from Immovable Property (Real Property)) through 19 (Students and Trainees)) of the Convention to the State of residence of the beneficial owner of the income. In order for an item of income to be "dealt with" in another article it must be the type of income described in the article and, in most cases, it must have its source in a Contracting State. For example, all royalty income that arises in a Contracting State and that is beneficially owned by a resident of the other Contracting State is "dealt with" in Article 12 (Royalties). However, profits derived in the conduct of a business are "dealt with" in Article 7 (Business Profits) whether or not they have their source in one of the Contracting States.

Examples of items of income covered by Article 20 include income from gambling, punitive (but not compensatory) damages and covenants not to compete. The article would also apply to income from a variety of financial transactions, where such income does not arise in the course of the conduct of a trade or business. For example, income from notional principal contracts and other derivatives would fall within Article 20 if derived by persons not engaged in the trade or business of dealing in such instruments, unless such instruments were being used to hedge risks arising in a trade or business. It would also apply to securities lending fees derived by an institutional investor. Further, in most cases guarantee fees paid within an intercompany group would be covered by Article 20, unless the guarantor were engaged in the business of providing such guarantees to unrelated parties.

Article 20 also applies to items of income that are not dealt with in the other articles because of their source or some other characteristic. For example, Article 11 (Interest) addresses only the taxation of interest arising in a Contracting State. Interest arising in a third State that is not attributable to a permanent establishment, therefore, is subject to Article 20.

Distributions from partnerships are not generally dealt with under Article 20 because partnership distributions generally do not constitute income. Under the Code, partners include in income their distributive share of partnership income annually, and partnership distributions themselves generally do not give rise to income. This would also be the case under U.S. law with respect to distributions from trusts. Trust income and distributions that, under the Code, have the character of the associated distributable net income would generally be covered by another article of the Convention. See Code section 641 et seq.

Paragraph 1

The general rule of Article 20 is contained in paragraph 1. Items of income not dealt with in other articles and beneficially owned by a resident of a Contracting State will be taxable only in the State of residence. This exclusive right of taxation applies whether or not the residence State exercises its right to tax the income covered by the Article.

The reference in this paragraph to "items of income beneficially owned by a resident of a Contracting State" rather than simply "items of income of a resident of a Contracting State," as in the OECD Model, is intended merely to make explicit the implicit understanding in other treaties that the exclusive residence taxation provided by paragraph 1 applies only when a resident of a Contracting State is the beneficial owner of the income. Thus, source taxation of income not dealt with in other articles of the Convention is not limited by paragraph 1 if it is nominally paid to a resident of the other Contracting State, but is beneficially owned by a resident of a third State. However, income received by a nominee on behalf of a resident of that other State would be entitled to benefits.

The term "beneficially owned" is not defined in the Convention, and is, therefore, defined as under the internal law of the country imposing tax (*i.e.*, the source country). The person who beneficially owns the income for purposes of Article 20 is the person to which the income is attributable for tax purposes under the laws of the source State.

Paragraph 2

This paragraph provides an exception to the general rule of paragraph 1 for income that is attributable to a permanent establishment maintained in a Contracting State by a resident of the other Contracting State. The taxation of such income is governed by the provisions of Article 7 (Business Profits). Therefore, income arising outside the United States that is paid in respect of a right or property that is effectively connected with a permanent establishment maintained in the United States by a resident of Iceland generally would be taxable by the United States under the provisions of Article 7. This would be true even if the income is sourced in a third state.

Relationship to Other Articles

This Article is subject to the saving clause of paragraph 4 of Article 1 (General Scope). Thus, the United States may tax the income of a resident of Iceland that is not dealt with elsewhere in the Convention, if that resident is a citizen of the United States. The Article is also subject to the provisions of Article 21 (Limitation On Benefits). Thus, if a resident of Iceland earns income that falls within the scope of paragraph 1 of Article 21, but that is taxable by the United States under U.S. law, the income would be exempt from U.S. tax under the provisions of Article 20 only if the resident satisfies one of the tests of Article 21 for entitlement to benefits.

ARTICLE 21 (LIMITATION ON BENEFITS)

Article 21 contains anti-treaty-shopping provisions that are intended to prevent residents of third countries from benefiting from what is intended to be a reciprocal agreement between two countries. In general, the provision does not rely on a determination of purpose or intention but instead sets forth a series of objective tests. A resident of a Contracting State that satisfies one of the tests will receive benefits regardless of its motivations in choosing its particular business structure.

The structure of the Article is as follows: Paragraph 1 states the general rule that residents are entitled to benefits otherwise accorded to residents only to the extent provided in the Article. Paragraph 2 lists a series of attributes of a resident of a Contracting State, the presence of any one of which will entitle that person to all the benefits of the Convention. Paragraph 3 provides a so-called "derivative benefits" test under which certain categories of income may qualify for benefits. Paragraph 4 provides that, regardless of whether a person qualifies for benefits under paragraph 2, benefits may be granted to that person with regard to certain income earned in the conduct of an active trade or business. Paragraph 5 provides special rules for so-called "triangular cases" notwithstanding the other provisions of Article 21. Paragraph 6 provides special rules for income from so-called "disproportionate shares" notwithstanding the other provisions of Article 21. Paragraph 7 provides that benefits also may be granted if the competent authority of the State from which benefits are claimed determines that it is appropriate to provide benefits in that case. Paragraph 8 defines certain terms used in the Article.

Paragraph 1

Paragraph 1 provides that a resident of a Contracting State will be entitled to the benefits otherwise accorded to residents of a Contracting State under the Convention only to the extent provided in the Article. The benefits otherwise accorded to residents under the Convention include all limitations on source-based taxation under Articles 6 (Income from Immovable Property (Real Property) through 20 (Other Income), the treaty-based relief from double taxation provided by Article 22 (Relief from Double Taxation), and the protection afforded to residents of a Contracting State under Article 23 (Non-Discrimination). Some provisions do not require that a person be a resident in order to enjoy the benefits of those provisions. Article 24 (Mutual Agreement Procedure) is not limited to residents of the Contracting States, and Article 26 (Members of Diplomatic Missions and Consular Posts) applies to diplomatic agents or consular officials regardless of residence. Article 21 accordingly does not limit the availability of treaty benefits under these provisions.

Article 21 and the anti-abuse provisions of domestic law complement each other, as Article 21 effectively determines whether an entity has a sufficient nexus to the Contracting State to be treated as a resident for treaty purposes, while domestic anti-abuse provisions (*e.g.*, business purpose, substance-over-form, step transaction or conduit principles) determine whether a particular transaction should be recast in accordance with its substance. Thus, internal law principles of the source Contracting State may be applied to identify the beneficial owner of an item of income, and Article 21 then will be applied to the beneficial owner to determine if that person is entitled to the benefits of the Convention with respect to such income.

Paragraph 2

Paragraph 2 has five subparagraphs, each of which describes a category of residents that are entitled to all benefits of the Convention.

It is intended that the provisions of paragraph 2 will be self executing. Unlike the provisions of paragraph 7, discussed below, claiming benefits under paragraph 2 does not require advance competent authority ruling or approval. The tax authorities may, of course, on review, determine that the taxpayer has improperly interpreted the paragraph and is not entitled to the benefits claimed.

Individuals -- Subparagraph 2(a)

Subparagraph 2(a) provides that individual residents of a Contracting State will be entitled to all treaty benefits. If such an individual receives income as a nominee on behalf of a third country resident, benefits may be denied under the respective articles of the Convention by the requirement that the beneficial owner of the income be a resident of a Contracting State.

Governments -- Subparagraph 2(b)

Subparagraph 2(b) provides that the Contracting States and any political subdivision or local authority thereof will be entitled to all benefits of the Convention.

Publicly-Traded Corporations -- Subparagraph 2(c)(i)

Subparagraph 2(c) applies to two categories of companies: publicly traded companies and subsidiaries of publicly traded companies. A company resident in a Contracting State is entitled to all the benefits of the Convention under clause (i) of subparagraph 2(c) if the principal class of its shares is regularly traded on one or more recognized stock exchanges and the company satisfies at least one of the following additional requirements: first, the company's principal class of shares is primarily traded on one or more recognized stock exchanges located in the Contracting State of which the company is a resident; or, second, the company's primary place of management and control is in its State of residence.

The term "recognized stock exchange" is defined in subparagraph 8(b). It includes (i) the NASDAQ System and any stock exchange registered with the Securities and Exchange Commission as a national securities exchange for purposes of the Securities Exchange Act of 1934; (ii) the Icelandic Stock Exchange; (iii) the stock exchanges of Amsterdam, Brussels, Copenhagen, Frankfurt, Hamburg, Helsinki, London, Oslo, Paris, Stockholm, Sydney, Tokyo, and Toronto; and (iv) any other stock exchange agreed upon by the competent authorities of the Contracting States.

If a company has only one class of shares, it is only necessary to consider whether the shares of that class meet the relevant trading requirements. If the company has more than one class of shares, it is necessary as an initial matter to determine which class or classes constitute the "principal class of shares". The term "principal class of shares" is defined in subparagraph 8(a) to mean the ordinary or common shares of the company representing the majority of the aggregate voting power and value of the company. If the company does not have a class of ordinary or common shares representing the majority of the aggregate voting power and value of the company, then the "principal class of shares" is that class or any combination of classes of shares that represents, in the aggregate, a majority of the voting power and value of the company. Although in a particular case involving a company with several classes of shares it is conceivable that more than one group of classes could be identified that account for more than 50% of the shares, it is only necessary for one such group to satisfy the requirements of this subparagraph in order for the company to be entitled to benefits. Benefits would not be denied to the company even if a second, non-qualifying, group of shares with more than half of the company's voting power and value could be identified.

The term "regularly traded" is not defined in the Convention. In accordance with paragraph 2 of Article 3 (General Definitions), this term will be defined by reference to the domestic tax laws of the State from which treaty benefits are sought, generally the source State. In the case of the United States, this term is understood to have the meaning it has under Treas. Reg. section 1.884-5(d)(4)(i)(B), relating to the branch tax provisions of the Code. Under these regulations, a class of shares is considered to be "regularly traded" if two requirements are met: trades in the class of shares are made in more than de minimis quantities on at least 60 days during the taxable year, and the aggregate number of shares in the class traded during the year is at least 10 percent of the average number of shares outstanding during the year. Sections 1.884-5(d)(4)(i)(A), (ii) and (iii) will not be taken into account for purposes of defining the term "regularly traded" under the Convention.

The regular trading requirement can be met by trading on any recognized exchange or exchanges located in either State. Trading on one or more recognized stock exchanges may be aggregated for purposes of this requirement. Thus, a U.S. company could satisfy the regularly traded requirement through trading, in whole or in part, on a recognized stock exchange located in Iceland. Authorized but unissued shares are not considered for purposes of this test.

The term "primarily traded" is not defined in the Convention. In accordance with paragraph 2 of Article 3, this term will have the meaning it has under the laws of the State concerning the taxes to which the Convention applies, generally the source State. In the case of the United States, this term is understood to have the meaning it has under Treas. Reg. section 1.884-5(d)(3), relating to the branch tax provisions of the Code. Accordingly, stock of a corporation is "primarily traded" if the number of shares in the company's principal class of shares that are traded during the taxable year on all recognized stock exchanges in the Contracting State of which the company is a resident exceeds the number of shares in the company's principal class of shares that are traded during that year on established securities markets in any other single foreign country.

A company whose principal class of shares is regularly traded on a recognized exchange but cannot meet the primarily traded test may claim treaty benefits if its primary place of management and control is in its country of residence. This test should be distinguished from the "place of effective management" test which is used in the OECD Model and by many other countries to establish residence. In some cases, the place of effective management test has been interpreted to mean the place where the board of directors meets. By contrast, the primary place of management and control test looks to where day-to-day responsibility for the management of the company (and its subsidiaries) is exercised. The company's primary place of management and control will be located in the State in which the company is a resident only if the executive officers and senior management employees exercise day-to-day responsibility for more of the strategic, financial and operational policy decision making for the company (including direct and indirect subsidiaries) in that State than in the other State or any third state, and the staff that support the management in making those decisions are also based in that State. Thus, the test looks to the overall activities of the relevant persons to see where those activities are conducted. In most cases, it will be a necessary, but not a sufficient, condition that the headquarters of the company (that is, the place at which the Chief Executive Officer and other top executives normally are based) be located in the Contracting State of which the company is a resident.

To apply the test, it will be necessary to determine which persons are to be considered "executive officers and senior management employees". In most cases, it will not be necessary to look beyond the executives who are members of the Board of Directors (the "inside directors") in the case of a U.S. company. That will not always be the case, however; in fact, the relevant persons may be employees of subsidiaries if those persons make the strategic, financial and operational policy decisions. Moreover, it would be necessary to take into account any special voting arrangements that result in certain board members making certain decisions without the participation of other board members.

Subsidiaries of Publicly-Traded Corporations -- Subparagraph 2(c)(ii)

A company resident in a Contracting State is entitled to all the benefits of the Convention under clause (ii) of subparagraph 2(c) if five or fewer publicly traded companies described in clause (i) are the direct or indirect owners of at least 50 percent of the aggregate vote and value of the company's shares. If the publicly-traded companies are indirect owners, however, each of the intermediate companies must be a resident of one of the Contracting States.

Thus, for example, a company that is a resident of Iceland, all the shares of which are owned by another company that is a resident of Iceland, would qualify for benefits under the Convention if the principal class of shares of the parent company are regularly and primarily traded on a recognized stock exchange in Iceland. However, such a subsidiary would not qualify for benefits under clause (ii) if the publicly traded parent company were a resident of a third state, for example, and not a resident of the United States or Iceland. Furthermore, if a parent company in Iceland indirectly owned the bottom-tier company through a chain of subsidiaries, each such subsidiary in the chain, as an intermediate owner, must be a resident of the United States or Iceland in order for the subsidiary to meet the test in clause (ii).

Tax Exempt Organizations -- Subparagraph 2(d)

Subparagraph 2(d) provides rules by which the tax exempt organizations described in paragraph 2 of Article 4 (Resident) will be entitled to all the benefits of the Convention. A pension scheme described in paragraph 2(a) of Article 4 or an employee benefits plan described in paragraph 2(b) of Article 4 will qualify for benefits if more than fifty percent of the beneficiaries, members or participants of the organization are individuals resident in either Contracting State. For purposes of this provision, the term "beneficiaries" should be understood to refer to the persons receiving benefits from the organization. On the other hand, an organization resident in a Contracting State that is established exclusively for religious, charitable, scientific, artistic, cultural, or educational purposes automatically qualifies for benefits, without regard to the residence of its beneficiaries or members.

Ownership/Base Erosion -- Subparagraph 2(e)

Subparagraph 2(e) provides an additional method to qualify for treaty benefits that applies to any form of legal entity that is a resident of a Contracting State. The test provided in subparagraph 2(e), the so-called ownership and base erosion test, is a two-part test. Both prongs of the test must be satisfied for the resident to be entitled to treaty benefits under subparagraph 2(e).

The ownership prong of the test, under clause (i), requires that 50 percent or more of each class of shares or other beneficial interests in the person is owned, directly or indirectly, on at least half the days of the person's taxable year by persons who are residents of the Contracting State of which that person is a resident and that are themselves entitled to treaty benefits under subparagraphs 2(a), 2(b), 2(d) or clause (i) of subparagraph 2(c). In the case of indirect owners, however, each of the intermediate owners must be a resident of that Contracting State.

Trusts may be entitled to benefits under this provision if they are treated as residents under Article 4 and they otherwise satisfy the requirements of this subparagraph. For purposes of this subparagraph, the beneficial interests in a trust will be considered to be owned by its beneficiaries in proportion to each beneficiary's actuarial interest in the trust. The interest of a remainder beneficiary will be equal to 100 percent less the aggregate percentages held by income beneficiaries. A beneficiary's interest in a trust will not be considered to be owned by a person entitled to benefits under subparagraphs 2(a), 2(b), 2(d) or clause (i) of subparagraph 2(c) if it is not possible to determine the beneficiary's actuarial interest. Consequently, if it is not possible to determine the actuarial interest of the beneficiaries in a trust, the ownership test under clause i) cannot be satisfied, unless all possible beneficiaries are persons entitled to benefits under subparagraphs 2(a), 2(b), 2(d) or clause (i) of subparagraph 2(c) .

The base erosion prong of clause (ii) of subparagraph 2(e) is satisfied with respect to a person if less than 50 percent of the person's gross income for the taxable year, as determined under the tax law in the person's State of residence, is paid or accrued, directly or indirectly, to persons who are not residents of either Contracting State entitled to benefits under subparagraphs 2(a), 2(b), 2(d) or clause (i) of subparagraph 2(c), in the form of payments deductible for tax purposes in the payer's State of residence. These amounts do not include arm's-length payments in the ordinary course of business for services or tangible property, or payments in respect of financial obligations to a bank, provided that where such a bank is not a resident of a Contracting State, such payment is attributable to a permanent establishment of that bank located in one of the Contracting States. To the extent they are deductible from the taxable base, trust distributions are deductible payments. However, depreciation and amortization deductions, which do not represent payments or accruals to other persons, are disregarded for this purpose.

Paragraph 3

Paragraph 3 sets forth a derivative benefits test that is potentially applicable to all treaty benefits, although the test is applied to individual items of income. In general, a derivative benefits test entitles the resident of a Contracting State to treaty benefits if the owner of the resident would have been entitled to the same benefit had the income in question flowed directly to that owner. To qualify under this paragraph, the company must meet an ownership test and a base erosion test.

56

Clause (i) of subparagraph 3(a) sets forth the ownership test. Under this test, at least 95 percent of the aggregate voting power and value of the shares of the company must be owned by seven or fewer persons that are residents of Member States of the European Union, or of the European Economic Area, or parties to the North American Free Trade Agreement or the European Free Trade Agreement. Ownership may be direct or indirect. To be considered a resident of Member States of the European Union, or of the European Economic Area, or parties to the North American Free Trade Agreement or the European Free Trade Agreement for purposes of paragraph 3, a person must meet the requirements of subparagraph 3(b). These requirements may be met in two alternative ways.

Under one alternative, a person may be treated as a resident of Member States of the European Union, or of the European Economic Area, or parties to the North American Free Trade Agreement or the European Free Trade Agreement because it is entitled to equivalent benefits under a treaty between the country of source and the country in which the person is a resident. To satisfy this requirement, the person must be entitled to all the benefits of a comprehensive income tax convention in force between the Contracting State from which benefits of the Convention are claimed and a qualifying state under provisions that are analogous to the rules in subparagraphs 2(a), 2(b), 2(d) and clause (i) of subparagraph 2(c). If the treaty in question does not have a comprehensive limitation on benefits article, this requirement is met only if the person would be entitled to treaty benefits under the tests in subparagraphs 2(a), 2(b), 2(d) and clause (i) of subparagraph 2(c) of this Article if the person were a resident of one of the Contracting States.

In order to satisfy this alternative with respect to dividends, interest, royalties or branch tax, the person must be entitled to a rate of tax that is at least as low as the tax rate that would apply under the Convention to such income. Thus, the rates to be compared are: (1) the rate of tax that the source State would have imposed if a qualified resident of the other Contracting State was the beneficial owner of the income; and (2) the rate of tax that the source State would have imposed if the third State resident received the income directly from the source State. For example, USCo is a wholly owned subsidiary of IceCo, a company resident in Iceland. IceCo is wholly owned by CanCo, a corporation resident in Canada. Assuming IceCo satisfies the requirements of paragraph 2 of Article 10 (Dividends), IceCo would be eligible for a dividend withholding tax rate of 5 percent. The dividend withholding tax rate in the treaty between the United States and Canada is also 5 percent. Thus, if CanCo received the dividend directly from USCo, CanCo would have been subject to a 5 percent rate of withholding tax on the dividend. Because CanCo would be entitled to a rate of withholding tax that is at least as low as the rate that would apply under the Convention to such income, CanCo is treated as a resident of Member States of the European Union, or of the European Economic Area, or parties to the North American Free Trade Agreement or the European Free Trade Agreement with respect to the elimination of withholding tax on dividends.

The requirement that a person be entitled to "all the benefits" of a comprehensive tax treaty eliminates those persons that qualify for benefits with respect to only certain types of income. Accordingly, the fact that a Canadian parent of an Icelandic company is engaged in the active conduct of a trade or business in Canada and therefore would be entitled to the benefits of the U.S.-Canada treaty if it received dividends directly from a U.S. subsidiary of the Icelandic company is not sufficient for purposes of this paragraph. Further, the Canadian company cannot be an equivalent beneficiary if it qualifies for benefits only with respect to certain income as a result of a "derivative benefits" provision in the U.S.-Canada treaty.

However, it would be possible to look through the Canadian company to its parent company to determine whether the parent company is an equivalent beneficiary.

The second alternative requirement for treatment as a resident of Member States of the European Union, or of the European Economic Area, or parties to the North American Free Trade Agreement or the European Free Trade Agreement is available only to residents of one of the two Contracting States. U.S. or Icelandic residents who are eligible for treaty benefits by reason of subparagraphs 2(a), 2(b), 2(d) or clause (i) of subparagraph 2(c) are treated as residents of Member States of the European Union, or of the European Economic Area, or parties to the North American Free Trade Agreement or the European Free Trade Agreement under the second alternative. Thus, an Icelandic individual will qualify without regard to whether the individual would have been entitled to receive the same benefits if it received the income directly. A resident of a third country cannot qualify for treaty benefits under any of those subparagraphs or any other rule of the treaty, and therefore does not qualify under this alternative. Thus, a resident of a third country will be treated as a resident of Member States of the European Union, or of the European Economic Area, or parties to the North American Free Trade Agreement or the European Free Trade Agreement only if it would have been entitled to equivalent benefits had it received the income directly.

The second alternative was included in order to clarify that ownership by certain residents of a Contracting State would not disqualify a U.S. or Icelandic company under this paragraph. Thus, for example, if 90 percent of an Icelandic company is owned by five companies that are resident in member states of the European Union who satisfy the requirements of clause (ii), and 10 percent of the Icelandic company is owned by a U.S. or Icelandic individual, then the Icelandic company still can satisfy the requirements of subparagraph 3(b).

Clause (ii) of subparagraph 3(a) sets forth the base erosion test. A company meets this base erosion test if less than 50 percent of its gross income (as determined in the company's State of residence) for the taxable period is paid or accrued, directly or indirectly, to a person or persons who are not residents of Member States of the European Union, or of the European Economic Area, or parties to the North American Free Trade Agreement or the European Free Trade Agreement in the form of payments deductible for tax purposes in company's State of residence.

Paragraph 4

Paragraph 4 sets forth an alternative test under which a resident of a Contracting State may receive treaty benefits with respect to certain items of income that are connected to an active trade or business conducted in its State of residence. A resident of a Contracting State may qualify for benefits under paragraph 4 whether or not it also qualifies under paragraph 2 or 3.

Subparagraph 4(a) sets forth the general rule that a resident of a Contracting State engaged in the active conduct of a trade or business in that State may obtain the benefits of the Convention with respect to an item of income derived in the other Contracting State. The item of income, however, must be derived in connection with or incidental to that trade or business.

The term "trade or business" is not defined in the Convention. Pursuant to paragraph 2 of Article 3 (General Definitions), when determining whether a resident of Iceland is entitled to the benefits of the Convention under paragraph 3 of this Article with respect to an item of income derived from sources within the United States, the United States will ascribe to this term the meaning that it has under the law of the United States. Accordingly, the U.S. competent authority will refer to the regulations issued under section 367(a) for the definition of the term "trade or business." In general, therefore, a trade or business will be considered to be a specific unified group of activities that constitute or could constitute an independent economic enterprise carried on for profit. Furthermore, a corporation generally will be considered to carry on a trade or business only if the officers and employees of the corporation conduct substantial managerial and operational activities.

The business of making or managing investments for the resident's own account will be considered to be a trade or business only when part of banking, insurance or securities activities conducted by a bank, an insurance company, or a registered securities dealer. Such activities conducted by a person other than a bank, insurance company or registered securities dealer will not be considered to be the conduct of an active trade or business, nor would they be considered to be the conduct of an active trade or business if conducted by a bank, insurance company or registered securities dealer but not as part of the company's banking, insurance or dealer business. Because a headquarters operation is in the business of managing investments, a company that functions solely as a headquarters company will not be considered to be engaged in an active trade or business for purposes of paragraph 3.

An item of income is derived in connection with a trade or business if the income-producing activity in the State of source is a line of business that "forms a part of" or is "complementary" to the trade or business conducted in the State of residence by the income recipient.

A business activity generally will be considered to form part of a business activity conducted in the State of source if the two activities involve the design, manufacture or sale of the same products or type of products, or the provision of similar services. The line of business in the State of residence may be upstream, downstream, or parallel to the activity conducted in the State of source. Thus, the line of business may provide inputs for a manufacturing process that occurs in the State of source, may sell the output of that manufacturing process, or simply may sell the same sorts of products that are being sold by the trade or business carried on in the State of source.

Example 1. USCo is a corporation resident in the United States. USCo is engaged in an active manufacturing business in the United States. USCo owns 100 percent of the shares of ICo, a corporation resident in Iceland. ICo distributes USCo products in Iceland. Since the business activities conducted by the two corporations involve the same products, ICo's distribution business is considered to form a part of USCo's manufacturing business.

Example 2. The facts are the same as in Example 1, except that USCo does not manufacture. Rather, USCo operates a large research and development facility in the United States that licenses intellectual property to affiliates worldwide, including ICo. ICo and other USCo affiliates then manufacture and market the USCo-designed products in their respective markets. Since the activities conducted by ICo and USCo involve the same product lines, these activities are considered to form a part of the same trade or business.

For two activities to be considered to be "complementary," the activities need not relate to the same types of products or services, but they should be part of the same overall industry and be related in the sense that the success or failure of one activity will tend to result in success or failure for the other. Where more than one trade or business is conducted in the State of source and only one of the trades or businesses forms a part of or is complementary to a trade or

59

business conducted in the State of residence, it is necessary to identify the trade or business to which an item of income is attributable. Royalties generally will be considered to be derived in connection with the trade or business to which the underlying intangible property is attributable. Dividends will be deemed to be derived first out of earnings and profits of the treaty-benefited trade or business, and then out of other earnings and profits. Interest income may be allocated under any reasonable method consistently applied. A method that conforms to U.S. principles for expense allocation will be considered a reasonable method.

Example 3. Americair is a corporation resident in the United States that operates an international airline. IceSub is a wholly-owned subsidiary of Americair resident in Iceland. IceSub operates a chain of hotels in Iceland that are located near airports served by Americair flights. Americair frequently sells tour packages that include air travel to Iceland and lodging at IceSub hotels. Although both companies are engaged in the active conduct of a trade or business, the businesses of operating a chain of hotels and operating an airline are distinct trades or businesses. Therefore IceSub's business does not form a part of Americair's business. However, IceSub's business is considered to be complementary to Americair's business because they are part of the same overall industry (travel) and the links between their operations tend to make them interdependent.

Example 4. The facts are the same as in Example 3, except that IceSub owns an office building in Iceland instead of a hotel chain. No part of Americair's business is conducted through the office building. IceSub's business is not considered to form a part of or to be complementary to Americair's business. They are engaged in distinct trades or businesses in separate industries, and there is no economic dependence between the two operations.

Example 5. USFlower is a corporation resident in the United States. USFlower produces and sells flowers in the United States and other countries. USFlower owns all the shares of IceHolding, a corporation resident in Iceland. IceHolding is a holding company that is not engaged in a trade or business. IceHolding owns all the shares of three corporations that are resident in Iceland: IceFlower, IceLawn, and IceFish. IceFlower distributes USFlower flowers under the USFlower trademark in Iceland. IceLawn markets a line of lawn care products in Iceland under the USFlower trademark. In addition to being sold under the same trademark, IceLawn and IceFlower products are sold in the same stores and sales of each company's products tend to generate increased sales of the other's products. IceFish imports fish from the United States and distributes it to fish wholesalers in Iceland. For purposes of paragraph 3, the business of IceFlower forms a part of the business of USFlower, the business of IceLawn is complementary to the business of USFlower, and the business of IceFish is neither part of nor complementary to that of USFlower.

An item of income derived from the State of source is "incidental to" the trade or business carried on in the State of residence if production of the item facilitates the conduct of the trade or business in the State of residence. An example of incidental income is the temporary investment of working capital of a person in the State of residence in securities issued by persons in the State of source.

Subparagraph 4(b) states a further condition to the general rule in subparagraph 4(a) in cases where the trade or business generating the item of income in question is carried on either by the person deriving the income or by any associated enterprises. Subparagraph 4(b) states that the trade or business carried on in the State of residence, under these circumstances, must be substantial in relation to the activity in the State of source. The substantiality requirement is intended to prevent a narrow case of treaty-shopping abuses in which a company attempts to qualify for benefits by engaging in de minimis connected business activities in the treaty country in which it is resident (*i.e.*, activities that have little economic cost or effect with respect to the company business as a whole).

The determination of substantiality is made based upon all the facts and circumstances and takes into account the comparative sizes of the trades or businesses in each Contracting State the nature of the activities performed in each Contracting State, and the relative contributions made to that trade or business in each Contracting State.

The determination in subparagraph 4(b) also is made separately for each item of income derived from the State of source. It therefore is possible that a person would be entitled to the benefits of the Convention with respect to one item of income but not with respect to another. If a resident of a Contracting State is entitled to treaty benefits with respect to a particular item of income under paragraph 3, the resident is entitled to all benefits of the Convention insofar as they affect the taxation of that item of income in the State of source.

Subparagraph 4(c) provides special attribution rules for purposes of applying the substantive rules of subparagraph 4(a). Thus, these rules apply for purposes of determining whether a person meets the requirement in subparagraph 4(a) that it be engaged in the active conduct of a trade or business and that the item of income is derived in connection with that active trade or business. Subparagraph 4(c) attributes to a person activities conducted by a partnership in which that person is a partner and activities conducted by persons "connected" to such person. A person ("X") is connected to another person ("Y") if X possesses 50 percent or more of the beneficial interest in Y (or if Y possesses 50 percent or more of the beneficial interest in X). For this purpose, X is connected to a company if X owns shares representing fifty percent or more of the aggregate voting power and value of the company or fifty percent or more of the beneficial equity interest in the company. X also is connected to Y if a third person possesses, directly or indirectly, fifty percent or more of the beneficial interest in both X and Y. For this purpose, if X or Y is a company, the threshold relationship with respect to such company or companies is fifty percent or more of the aggregate voting power and value or fifty percent or more of the beneficial equity interest. Finally, X is connected to Y if, based upon all the facts and circumstances, X controls Y, Y controls X, or X and Y are controlled by the same person or persons.

Paragraph 5

Paragraph 5 deals with the treatment of income in the context of a so-called "triangular case."

The term "triangular case" refers to the use of the following structure by a resident of Iceland to earn, in this case, interest income from the United States. The resident of Iceland, who is assumed to qualify for benefits under one or more of the provisions of Article 16 (Limitation on Benefits), sets up a permanent establishment in a third jurisdiction that imposes only a low rate of tax on the income of the permanent establishment. The Icelandic resident lends funds into the United States through the permanent establishment. The permanent establishment, despite its third-jurisdiction location, is an integral part of a Icelandic resident. Therefore the income that it earns on those loans, absent the provisions of paragraph 5, is entitled to exemption from U.S. withholding tax under the Convention. Under a current Icelandic income tax treaty with the host jurisdiction of the permanent establishment, the income of the permanent establishment is exempt from Icelandic tax (alternatively, Iceland may choose to exempt the income of the permanent establishment from Icelandic income tax). Thus, the interest income is exempt from

U.S. tax, is subject to little tax in the host jurisdiction of the permanent establishment, and is exempt from Icelandic tax.

Paragraph 5 applies reciprocally. However, the United States does not exempt the profits of a third-jurisdiction permanent establishment of a U.S. resident from U.S. tax, either by statute or by treaty.

Paragraph 5 provides that the tax benefits that would otherwise apply under the Convention will not apply to any item of income if the combined tax actually paid in the residence State and the third state is less than 60 percent of the tax that would have been payable in the residence State if the income were earned in that State by the enterprise and were not attributable to the permanent establishment in the third state. In the case of dividends, interest and royalties to which this paragraph applies, the withholding tax rates under the Convention are replaced with a 15 percent withholding tax. Any other income to which the provisions of paragraph 5 apply is subject to tax under the domestic law of the source State, notwithstanding any other provisions of the Convention.

In general, the principles employed under Code section 954(b)(4) will be employed to determine whether the profits are subject to an effective rate of taxation that is above the specified threshold.

Notwithstanding the level of tax on interest and royalty income of the permanent establishment, paragraph 5 will not apply under certain circumstances. In the case of royalties, paragraph 5 will not apply if the royalties are received as compensation for the use of, or the right to use, intangible property produced or developed by the permanent establishment itself. In the case of any other income, paragraph 5 will not apply if that income is derived in connection with, or is incidental to, the active conduct of a trade or business carried on by the permanent establishment in the third state. The business of making, managing or simply holding investments is not considered to be an active trade or business, unless these are banking or securities activities carried on by a bank or registered securities dealer.

Paragraph 6

Paragraph 6 provides a special rule where a company resident in a Contracting State, or a company that controls such a company directly or indirectly, has a class of shares that is subject to terms or other arrangements that entitle the holder to a larger portion of the company's income than the portion the holders would receive absent such terms or arrangements ("the disproportionate part of the income"). Where 50 percent or more of such a class of shares is owned by persons who are not entitled to benefits under paragraph 2, the benefits of the Convention shall not apply with respect to the disproportionate part of the income of the Company.

The following example illustrates this result.

Example. IceCo is a corporation resident in Iceland. IceCo has two classes of shares: Common and Preferred. The Common shares are listed and regularly traded on the Icelandic Stock Exchange. The Preferred shares have no voting rights and are entitled to receive dividends equal in amount to interest payments that IceCo receives from unrelated borrowers in the United States. The Preferred shares are owned entirely by a single investor that is a resident of a third country. The Common shares account for more than 50 percent of the value of IceCo and for 100 percent of the voting power. Because the owner of the Preferred shares is entitled to receive payments corresponding to the U.S. source interest income earned by IceCo, the Preferred shares are a disproportionate class of shares. Because the Preferred shares are not owned by persons entitled to benefits under paragraph 2, the benefits of the Convention shall not apply with respect to IceCo's U.S.-source interest income.

Paragraph 7

Paragraph 7 provides that a resident of one of the States that is not entitled to the benefits of the Convention as a result of paragraphs 1 through 5 still shall be granted benefits under the Convention if the competent authority of the State from which benefits are claimed determines that the establishment, acquisition, or maintenance of the person seeking benefits under the Convention, or the conduct of such person's operations, has or had as one of its principal purposes the obtaining of benefits under the Convention. Benefits will not be granted, however, solely because a company was established prior to the effective date of a treaty or protocol. In that case a company would still be required to establish, to the satisfaction of the competent authority, clear non-tax business reasons for its formation in a Contracting State, or that the allowance of benefits would not otherwise be contrary to the purposes of the treaty. Thus, persons that establish operations in one of the States with a principal purpose of obtaining the benefits of the Convention ordinarily will not be granted relief under paragraph 7.

The competent authority's discretion is quite broad. It may grant all of the benefits of the Convention to the taxpayer making the request, or it may grant only certain benefits. For instance, it may grant benefits only with respect to a particular item of income in a manner similar to paragraph 3. Further, the competent authority may establish conditions, such as setting time limits on the duration of any relief granted.

For purposes of implementing paragraph 7, a taxpayer will be permitted to present his case to the relevant competent authority for an advance determination based on the facts. In these circumstances, it is also expected that, if the competent authority determines that benefits are to be allowed, they will be allowed retroactively to the time of entry into force of the relevant treaty provision or the establishment of the structure in question, whichever is later.

Finally, there may be cases in which a resident of a Contracting State may apply for discretionary relief to the competent authority of his State of residence. This would arise, for example, if the benefit it is claiming is provided by the residence country, and not by the source country. So, for example, if a company that is a resident of the United States would like to claim the benefit of the re-sourcing rule of subparagraph 2(a) of Article 22, but it does not meet any of the objective tests of paragraphs 2 through 5, it may apply to the U.S. competent authority for discretionary relief.

Paragraph 8

Paragraph 8 defines several key terms for purposes of Article 22. Each of the defined terms is discussed above in the context in which it is used.

ARTICLE 22 (RELIEF FROM DOUBLE TAXATION)

This Article describes the manner in which each Contracting State undertakes to relieve double taxation. The United States uses the foreign tax credit method under its internal law, and by treaty.

Paragraph 1

The United States agrees, in paragraph 1, to allow to its citizens and residents a credit against U.S. tax for income taxes paid or accrued to Iceland. Paragraph 1 also provides that Iceland's covered taxes are income taxes for U.S. purposes. This provision is based on the Treasury Department's review of Iceland's laws.

Subparagraph 1(b) provides for a deemed-paid credit, consistent with section 902 of the Code, to a U.S. corporation in respect of dividends received from a corporation resident in Iceland of which the U.S. corporation owns at least 10 percent of the voting stock. This credit is for the tax paid by the corporation to Iceland on the profits out of which the dividends are considered paid.

The credits allowed under paragraph 1 are allowed in accordance with the provisions and subject to the limitations of U.S. law, as that law may be amended over time, so long as the general principle of the Article, that is, the allowance of a credit, is retained. Thus, although the Convention provides for a foreign tax credit, the terms of the credit are determined by the provisions, at the time a credit is given, of the U.S. statutory credit.

Therefore, the U.S. credit under the Convention is subject to the various limitations of U.S. law (see, *e.g.*, Code sections 901-908). For example, the credit against U.S. tax generally is limited to the amount of U.S. tax due with respect to net foreign source income within the relevant foreign tax credit limitation category (see Code section 904(a) and (d)), and the dollar amount of the credit is determined in accordance with U.S. currency translation rules (see, *e.g.*, Code section 986). Similarly, U.S. law applies to determine carryover periods for excess credits and other inter-year adjustments.

Paragraph 2

Paragraph 2 provides a re-sourcing rule for gross income covered by paragraph 1. Subparagraph 2(a) is intended to ensure that a U.S. resident can obtain an appropriate amount of U.S. foreign tax credit for income taxes paid to Iceland when the Convention assigns to Iceland primary taxing rights over an item of gross income.

Accordingly, if the Convention allows Iceland to tax an item of gross income (as defined under U.S. law) derived by a resident of the United States, the United States will treat that item of gross income as gross income from sources within Iceland for U.S. foreign tax credit purposes. In the case of a U.S.-owned foreign corporation, however, section 904(g)(10) may apply for purposes of determining the U.S. foreign tax credit with respect to income subject to this re-sourcing rule. Section 904(g)(10) generally applies the foreign tax credit limitation separately to re-sourced income. Furthermore, the subparagraph 2(a) re-sourcing rule applies to gross income, not net income. Accordingly, U.S. expense allocation and apportionment rules, see, *e.g.*, Treas. Reg. section 1.861-9, continue to apply to income resourced under subparagraph 2(a).

Subparagraph 2(b) provides that gains derived by an individual who was a resident of the United States that are taxed by the United States in accordance with the Convention, and that may also be taxed in Iceland solely by reason of Article 13 (Capital Gains), shall be deemed to be gains from sources in the United States. The provisions of subparagraph 2(b) ensure that the United States does not bear, from a foreign tax credit standpoint, the cost of Iceland's expatriation tax.

Paragraph 3

Specific rules are provided in paragraph 3 under which Iceland, in imposing tax on its residents, provides relief for U.S. taxes paid by those residents. Subparagraph 3(a) provides that when a resident of Iceland derives income that, in accordance with the provisions of the Convention, may be taxed in the United States, Iceland shall allow as a credit against Icelandic income taxes an amount equal to those taxes paid to the United States.

Subparagraph 3(b) limits the credits against Icelandic taxes to those taxes that are attributable to the income that has been taxed by the United States.

Subparagraph 3(c) provides that when a resident of Iceland derives income that, in accordance with the provisions of the Convention, may be taxed by the United States, Iceland shall allow the credit against Icelandic tax described in subparagraph 3(b). However, subparagraph 3(c) also permits Iceland to include the income corresponding to the U.S. tax in the resident's tax base for purposes of determining the Icelandic tax. This rule is a variation of the "exemption with progression rule," adapted to accommodate Iceland's credit system. It is also similar to U.S. domestic law, which permits credits for foreign taxes paid, while at the same time taxing residents on worldwide income. Finally, subparagraph 3(c) provides that for purposes of this Article, the U.S. taxes referred to in subparagraph 3(b) and paragraph 4 of Article 2 (Taxes Covered) are considered to be income taxes and are allowed as credits against Icelandic tax on income, subject to all of the provisions and limitations of this paragraph.

Paragraph 4

Paragraph 4 provides special rules for the tax treatment in both States of certain types of income derived from U.S. sources by U.S. citizens who are residents of Iceland. Since U.S. citizens, regardless of residence, are subject to United States tax at ordinary progressive rates on their worldwide income, the U.S. tax on the U.S. source income of a U.S. citizen resident in Iceland may exceed the U.S. tax that may be imposed under the Convention on an item of U.S. source income derived by a resident of Iceland who is not a U.S. citizen. The provisions of paragraph 4 ensure that Iceland does not bear the cost of U.S. taxation of its citizens who are residents of Iceland.

Subparagraph 4(a) provides, with respect to items of income from sources within the United States, special credit rules for Iceland. These rules apply to items of U.S.-source income that would be either exempt from U.S. tax or subject to reduced rates of U.S. tax under the provisions of the Convention if they had been received by a resident of Iceland who is not a U.S. citizen. The tax credit allowed under paragraph 4 with respect to such items need not exceed the U.S. tax that may be imposed under the Convention, other than tax imposed solely by reason of the U.S. citizenship of the taxpayer under the provisions of the saving clause of paragraph 4 of Article 1 (General Scope).

For example, if a U.S. citizen resident in Iceland receives portfolio dividends from sources within the United States, the foreign tax credit granted by Iceland would be limited to 15 percent of the dividend – the U.S. tax that may be imposed under subparagraph 2(b) of Article 10 (Dividends) – even if the shareholder is subject to U.S. net income tax because of his U.S. citizenship. With respect to interest income, Iceland would allow no foreign tax credit, because its residents are exempt from U.S. tax on interest income under the provisions of Articles 11 (Interest).

Subparagraph 4(b) eliminates the potential for double taxation that can arise because subparagraph 4(a) provides that Iceland need not provide full relief for the U.S. tax imposed on its citizens resident in Iceland. The subparagraph provides that the United States will credit the income tax paid or accrued to Iceland, after the application of subparagraph 4(a). It further provides that in allowing the credit, the United States will not reduce its tax below the amount that is taken into account in Iceland in applying subparagraph 4(a).

Since the income described in subparagraph 4(a) generally will be U.S. source income, special rules are required to re-source some of the income to Iceland in order for the United States to be able to credit the tax paid to Iceland. This re-sourcing is provided for in subparagraph 4(c), which deems the items of income referred to in subparagraph 4(a) to be from foreign sources to the extent necessary to avoid double taxation under subparagraph 4(b). Clause (iii) of subparagraph 3(c) of Article 24 (Mutual Agreement Procedure) provides a mechanism by which the competent authorities can resolve any disputes regarding whether income is from sources within the United States.

The following two examples illustrate the application of paragraph 4 in the case of a U.S.-source portfolio dividend received by a U.S. citizen resident in Iceland. In both examples, the U.S. rate of tax on residents of Iceland, under subparagraph 2(b) of Article 10 (Dividends) of the Convention, is 15 percent. In both examples, the U.S. income tax rate on the U.S. citizen is 35 percent. In example 1, the rate of income tax imposed in Iceland on its resident (the U.S. citizen) is 25 percent (below the U.S. rate), and in example 2, the rate imposed on its resident is 40 percent (above the U.S. rate).

Subparagraph (a)	Example 1	Example 2
U.S. dividend declared	$100.00	$100.00
Notional U.S. withholding tax (Article 10(2)(b))	15.00	15.00
Taxable income in Iceland	100.00	100.00
Icelandic tax before credit	25.00	40.00
Less: tax credit for notional U.S. withholding tax	15.00	15.00
Net post-credit tax paid to Iceland	10.00	25.00

Subparagraphs (b) and (c)	Example 1	Example 2
U.S. pre-tax income	$100.00	$100.00
U.S. pre-credit citizenship tax	35.00	35.00
Notional U.S. withholding tax	15.00	15.00
U.S. tax eligible to be offset by credit	20.00	20.00
Tax paid to Iceland	10.00	25.00
Income re-sourced from U.S. to foreign source (see below)	28.57	57.14
U.S. pre-credit tax on re-sourced income	10.00	20.00
U.S. credit for tax paid to Iceland	10.00	20.00
Net post-credit U.S. tax	10.00	0.00
Total U.S. tax	25.00	15.00

In both examples, in the application of subparagraph 4(a), Iceland credits a 15 percent U.S. tax against its residence tax on the U.S. citizen. In the first example, the net tax paid to Iceland after the foreign tax credit is $10.00; in the second example, it is $25.00. In the application of subparagraphs 4(b) and 4(c), from the U.S. tax due before credit of $35.00, the United States subtracts the amount of the U.S. source tax of $15.00, against which no U.S. foreign tax credit is allowed. This subtraction ensures that the United States collects the tax that it is due under the Convention as the State of source.

In both examples, given the 35 percent U.S. tax rate, the maximum amount of U.S. tax against which credit for the tax paid to Iceland may be claimed is $20 ($35 U.S. tax minus $15 U.S. withholding tax). Initially, all of the income in both examples was from sources within the United States. For a U.S. foreign tax credit to be allowed for the full amount of the tax paid to Iceland, an appropriate amount of the income must be re-sourced to Iceland under subparagraph 4(c).

The amount that must be re-sourced depends on the amount of tax for which the U.S. citizen is claiming a U.S. foreign tax credit. In example 1, the tax paid to Iceland was $10. For this amount to be creditable against U.S. tax, $28.57 ($10 tax divided by 35 percent U.S. tax rate) must be resourced to Iceland. When the tax is credited against the $10 of U.S. tax on this resourced income, there is a net U.S. tax of $10 due after credit ($20 U.S. tax eligible to be offset by credit, minus $10 tax paid to Iceland). Thus, in example 1, there is a total of $25 in U.S. tax ($15 U.S. withholding tax plus $10 residual U.S. tax).

In example 2, the tax paid to Iceland was $25, but, because the United States subtracts the U.S. withholding tax of $15 from the total U.S. tax of $35, only $20 of U.S. taxes may be offset by taxes paid to Iceland. Accordingly, the amount that must be resourced to Iceland is limited to the amount necessary to ensure a U.S. foreign tax credit for $20 of tax paid to Iceland, or $57.14 ($20 tax paid to Iceland divided by 35 percent U.S. tax rate). When the tax paid to Iceland is credited against the U.S. tax on this re-sourced income, there is no residual U.S. tax ($20 U.S. tax minus $25 tax paid to Iceland, subject to the U.S. limit of $20). Thus, in example 2, there is a total of $15 in U.S. tax ($15 U.S. withholding tax plus $0 residual U.S. tax). Because the tax paid to Iceland was $25 and the U.S. tax eligible to be offset by credit was $20, there is $5 of excess foreign tax credit available for carryover.

Relationship to other Articles

By virtue of subparagraph 5(a) of Article 1 (General Scope), Article 22 is not subject to the saving clause of paragraph 4 of Article 1. Thus, the United States will allow a credit to its citizens and residents in accordance with the Article, even if such credit were to provide a benefit not available under the Code (such as the re-sourcing provided by paragraph 2 and subparagraph 4(c)).

ARTICLE 23 (NON-DISCRIMINATION)

This Article ensures that nationals of a Contracting State, in the case of paragraph 1, and residents of a Contracting State, in the case of paragraphs 2 through 4, will not be subject, directly or indirectly, to discriminatory taxation in the other Contracting State. Not all differences in tax treatment, either as between nationals of the two States, or between residents of the two States, are violations of the prohibition against discrimination. Rather, the non-discrimination obligations of this Article apply only if the nationals or residents of the two States are comparably situated.

Each of the relevant paragraphs of the Article provides that two persons that are comparably situated must be treated similarly. Although the actual words differ from paragraph to paragraph (*e.g.*, paragraph 1 refers to two nationals "in the same circumstances," paragraph 2 refers to two enterprises "carrying on the same activities" and paragraph 4 refers to two enterprises that are "similar"), the common underlying premise is that if the difference in treatment is directly related to a tax-relevant difference in the situations of the domestic and foreign persons being compared, that difference is not to be treated as discriminatory (i.e., if one person is taxable in a Contracting State on worldwide income and the other is not, or tax may be collectible from one person at a later stage, but not from the other, distinctions in treatment would be justified under paragraph 1). Other examples of such factors that can lead to non-discriminatory differences in treatment are noted in the discussions of each paragraph.

The operative paragraphs of the Article also use different language to identify the kinds of differences in taxation treatment that will be considered discriminatory. For example, paragraphs 1 and 4 speak of "any taxation or any requirement connected therewith that is more burdensome," while paragraph 2 specifies that a tax "shall not be less favorably levied." Regardless of these differences in language, only differences in tax treatment that materially disadvantage the foreign person relative to the domestic person are properly the subject of the Article.

Paragraph 1

Paragraph 1 provides that a national of one Contracting State may not be subject to taxation or connected requirements in the other Contracting State that are different from or more burdensome than the taxes and connected requirements imposed upon a national of that other State in the same circumstances.

The term "national" in relation to a Contracting State is defined in subparagraph 1(j) of Article 3 (General Definitions). The term includes both individuals and juridical persons. A national of a Contracting State is afforded protection under this paragraph even if the national is not a resident of either Contracting State. Thus, a U.S. citizen who is resident in a third country is entitled, under this paragraph, to the same treatment in Iceland as a national of Iceland who is in similar circumstances (i.e., presumably one who is resident in a third State).

As noted above, whether or not the two persons are both taxable on worldwide income is a significant circumstance for this purpose. For this reason, paragraph 1 specifically states that the United States is not obligated to apply the same taxing regime to a national of Iceland who is not resident in the United States as it applies to a U.S. national who is not resident in the United States. United States citizens who are not residents of the United States but who are, nevertheless, subject to United States tax on their worldwide income are not in the same circumstances with respect to United States taxation as citizens of Iceland who are not United States residents. Thus, for example, Article 23 would not entitle a national of Iceland resident in a third country to taxation at graduated rates on U.S. source dividends or other investment income that applies to a U.S. citizen resident in the same third country.

Paragraph 2

Paragraph 2 of the Article, provides that a Contracting State may not tax a permanent establishment of an enterprise of the other Contracting State less favorably than an enterprise of that first-mentioned State that is carrying on the same activities.

The fact that a U.S. permanent establishment of an enterprise of Iceland is subject to U.S. tax only on income that is attributable to the permanent establishment, while a U.S. corporation engaged in the same activities is taxable on its worldwide income is not, in itself, a sufficient difference to provide different treatment for the permanent establishment. There are cases, however, where the two enterprises would not be similarly situated and differences in treatment may be warranted. For instance, it would not be a violation of the non-discrimination protection of paragraph 2 to require the foreign enterprise to provide information in a reasonable manner that may be different from the information requirements imposed on a resident enterprise, because information may not be as readily available to the Internal Revenue Service from a foreign as from a domestic enterprise. Similarly, it would not be a violation of paragraph 2 to impose penalties on persons who fail to comply with such a requirement (see, *e.g.*, sections 874(a) and 882(c)(2)). Further, a determination that income and expenses have been attributed or allocated to a permanent establishment in conformity with the principles of Article 7 (Business Profits) implies that the attribution or allocation was not discriminatory.

Section 1446 of the Code imposes on any partnership with income that is effectively connected with a U.S. trade or business the obligation to withhold tax on amounts allocable to a foreign partner. In the context of the Convention, this obligation applies with respect to a share of the partnership income of a partner resident in Iceland, and attributable to a U.S. permanent establishment. There is no similar obligation with respect to the distributive shares of U.S. resident partners. It is understood, however, that this distinction is not a form of discrimination within the meaning of paragraph 2 of the Article. No distinction is made between U.S. and non-U.S. partnerships, since the law requires that partnerships of both U.S. and non-U.S. domicile withhold tax in respect of the partnership shares of non-U.S. partners. Furthermore, in distinguishing between U.S. and non-U.S. partners, the requirement to withhold on the non-U.S. but not the U.S. partner's share is not discriminatory taxation, but, like other withholding on nonresident aliens, is merely a reasonable method for the collection of tax from persons who are not continually present in the United States, and as to whom it otherwise may be difficult for the United States to enforce its tax jurisdiction. If tax has been over-withheld, the partner can, as in other cases of over-withholding, file for a refund.

Paragraph 2 does not obligate a Contracting State to grant to a resident of the other Contracting State any tax allowances, reliefs, etc., that it grants to its own residents on account of their civil status or family responsibilities. Thus, if a sole proprietor who is a resident of Iceland has a permanent establishment in the United States, in assessing income tax on the profits attributable to the permanent establishment, the United States is not obligated to allow to the resident of Iceland the personal allowances for himself and his family that he would be permitted to take if the permanent establishment were a sole proprietorship owned and operated by a U.S. resident, despite the fact that the individual income tax rates would apply.

Paragraph 3

Paragraph 3 prohibits discrimination in the allowance of deductions. When a resident or an enterprise of a Contracting State pays interest, royalties or other disbursements to a resident of the other Contracting State, the first-mentioned Contracting State must allow a deduction for those payments in computing the taxable profits of the resident or enterprise as if the payment had been made under the same conditions to a resident of the first-mentioned Contracting State. Paragraph 3, however, does not require a Contracting State to give nonresidents more favorable treatment than it gives to its own residents. Consequently, a Contracting State does not have to allow nonresidents a deduction for items that are not deductible under its domestic law (for example, expenses of a capital nature).

The term "other disbursements" is understood to include a reasonable allocation of executive and general administrative expenses, research and development expenses and other expenses incurred for the benefit of a group of related persons that includes the person incurring the expense.

An exception to the rule of paragraph 3 is provided for cases where the provisions of paragraph 1 of Article 9 (Associated Enterprises), paragraph 4 of Article 11 (Interest) or paragraph 6 of Article 12 (Royalties) apply. All of these provisions permit the denial of deductions in certain circumstances in respect of transactions between related persons. Neither State is forced to apply the non-discrimination principle in such cases. The exception with respect to paragraph 4 of Article 11 would include the denial or deferral of certain interest deductions under Code section 163(j).

Paragraph 3 also provides that any debts of an enterprise of a Contracting State to a resident of the other Contracting State are deductible in the first-mentioned Contracting State for purposes of computing the capital tax of the enterprise under the same conditions as if the debt had been contracted to a resident of the first-mentioned Contracting State. Even though, for general purposes, the Convention covers only income taxes, under paragraph 6 of this Article, the nondiscrimination provisions apply to all taxes levied in both Contracting States, at all levels of government.

Paragraph 4

Paragraph 4 requires that a Contracting State not impose more burdensome taxation or connected requirements on an enterprise of that State that is wholly or partly owned or controlled, directly or indirectly, by one or more residents of the other Contracting State than the taxation or connected requirements that it imposes on other similar enterprises of that first-mentioned Contracting State. For this purpose it is understood that "similar" refers to similar activities or ownership of the enterprise.

This rule, like all non-discrimination provisions, does not prohibit differing treatment of entities that are in differing circumstances. Rather, a protected enterprise is only required to be treated in the same manner as other enterprises that, from the point of view of the application of the tax law, are in substantially similar circumstances both in law and in fact. The taxation of a distributing corporation under section 367(e) on an applicable distribution to foreign shareholders does not violate paragraph 4 of the Article because a foreign-owned corporation is not similar to a domestically-owned corporation that is accorded non-recognition treatment under sections 337 and 355.

For the reasons given above in connection with the discussion of paragraph 2 of the Article, it is also understood that the provision in section 1446 of the Code for withholding of tax on non-U.S. partners does not violate paragraph 5 of the Article.

It is further understood that the ineligibility of a U.S. corporation with nonresident alien shareholders to make an election to be an "S" corporation does not violate paragraph 4 of the Article. If a corporation elects to be an S corporation, it is generally not subject to income tax and the shareholders take into account their pro rata shares of the corporation's items of income, loss, deduction or credit. (The purpose of the provision is to allow an individual or small group of individuals the protections of conducting business in corporate form while paying taxes at individual rates as if the business were conducted directly.) A nonresident alien does not pay U.S. tax on a net basis, and, thus, does not generally take into account items of loss, deduction or credit. Thus, the S corporation provisions do not exclude corporations with nonresident alien shareholders because such shareholders are foreign, but only because they are not net-basis taxpayers. Similarly, the provisions exclude corporations with other types of shareholders where the purpose of the provisions cannot be fulfilled or their mechanics implemented. For example, corporations with corporate shareholders are excluded because the purpose of the provision to permit individuals to conduct a business in corporate form at individual tax rates would not be furthered by their inclusion.

Finally, it is understood that paragraph 4 does not require a Contracting State to allow foreign corporations to join in filing a consolidated return with a domestic corporation or to allow similar benefits between domestic and foreign enterprises.

Paragraph 5

Paragraph 5 of the Article confirms that no provision of the Article will prevent either Contracting State from imposing the branch profits tax described in paragraph 8 of Article 10 (Dividends).

Paragraph 6

As noted above, notwithstanding the specification of taxes covered by the Convention in Article 2 (Taxes Covered) for general purposes, for purposes of providing nondiscrimination protection this Article applies to taxes of every kind and description imposed by a Contracting State or a political subdivision or local authority thereof. Customs duties are not considered to be taxes for this purpose.

Relationship to Other Articles

The saving clause of paragraph 4 of Article 1 (General Scope) does not apply to this Article by virtue of the exceptions in subparagraph 5(a) of Article 1. Thus, for example, a U.S. citizen who is a resident of Iceland may claim benefits in the United States under this Article.

Nationals of a Contracting State may claim the benefits of paragraph 1 regardless of whether they are entitled to benefits under Article 21 (Limitation on Benefits), because that paragraph applies to nationals and not residents. They may not claim the benefits of the other paragraphs of this Article with respect to an item of income unless they are generally entitled to treaty benefits with respect to that income under a provision of Article 21.

ARTICLE 24 (MUTUAL AGREEMENT PROCEDURE)

This Article provides the mechanism for taxpayers to bring to the attention of competent authorities issues and problems that may arise under the Convention. It also provides the authority for cooperation between the competent authorities of the Contracting States to resolve disputes and clarify issues that may arise under the Convention and to resolve cases of double taxation not provided for in the Convention. The competent authorities of the two Contracting States are identified in subparagraph 1(i) of Article 3 (General Definitions).

Paragraph 1

This paragraph provides that where a resident of a Contracting State considers that the actions of one or both Contracting States will result in taxation that is not in accordance with the

Convention, he may present his case to the competent authority of either Contracting State. This rule is more generous than in most treaties, which generally allow taxpayers to bring competent authority cases only to the competent authority of their country of residence, or citizenship/nationality. Under this more generous rule, a U.S. permanent establishment of a corporation resident in Iceland that faces inconsistent treatment in the two countries would be able to bring its request for assistance to the U.S. competent authority. If the U.S. competent authority can resolve the issue on its own, then the taxpayer need never involve the Icelandic competent authority. Thus, the rule provides flexibility that might result in greater efficiency.

Although the typical cases brought under this paragraph will involve economic double taxation arising from transfer pricing adjustments, the scope of this paragraph is not limited to such cases. For example, a taxpayer could request assistance from the competent authority if one Contracting State determines that the taxpayer has received deferred compensation taxable at source under Article 14 (Income from Employment), while the taxpayer believes that such income should be treated as a pension that is taxable only in his country of residence pursuant to Article 17 (Pensions, Social Security, and Annuities).

It is not necessary for a person requesting assistance first to have exhausted the remedies provided under the national laws of the Contracting States before presenting a case to the competent authorities, nor does the fact that the statute of limitations may have passed for seeking a refund preclude bringing a case to the competent authority. Unlike the OECD Model, no time limit is provided within which a case must be brought.

Paragraph 2

Paragraph 2 sets out the framework within which the competent authorities will deal with cases brought by taxpayers under paragraph 1. It provides that, if the competent authority of the Contracting State to which the case is presented judges the case to have merit, and cannot reach a unilateral solution, it shall seek an agreement with the competent authority of the other Contracting State pursuant to which taxation not in accordance with the Convention will be avoided.

Any agreement is to be implemented even if such implementation otherwise would be barred by the statute of limitations or by some other procedural limitation, such as a closing agreement. Paragraph 2, however, does not prevent the application of domestic-law procedural limitations that give effect to the agreement (*e.g.*, a domestic-law requirement that the taxpayer file a return reflecting the agreement within one year of the date of the agreement).

Where the taxpayer has entered a closing agreement (or other written settlement) with the United States before bringing a case to the competent authorities, the U.S. competent authority will endeavor only to obtain a correlative adjustment from Iceland. *See* Rev. Proc. 2006-54, 2006-49 I.R.B. 1035, § 7.05. Because, as specified in paragraph 2 of Article 1 (General Scope), the Convention cannot operate to increase a taxpayer's liability, temporal or other procedural limitations can be overridden only for the purpose of making refunds and not to impose additional tax.

Paragraph 3

Paragraph 3 authorizes the competent authorities to resolve difficulties or doubts that may arise as to the application or interpretation of the Convention. The paragraph includes a non- exhaustive list of examples of the kinds of matters about which the competent authorities may reach agreement. This list is purely illustrative; it does not grant any authority that is not implicitly present as a result of the introductory sentence of paragraph 3.

The competent authorities may, for example, agree to the same allocation of income, deductions, credits or allowances between an enterprise in one Contracting State and its permanent establishment in the other or between related persons. These allocations are to be made in accordance with the arm's length principle underlying Article 7 (Business Profits) and Article 9 (Associated Enterprises). Agreements reached under these subparagraphs may include agreement on a methodology for determining an appropriate transfer price, on an acceptable range of results under that methodology, or on a common treatment of a taxpayer's cost sharing arrangement.

As indicated in subparagraphs 3(a) through 3(f), the competent authorities also may agree to settle a variety of conflicting applications of the Convention. They may agree to settle conflicts regarding the characterization of particular items of income, including the same characterization of income that is assimilated to income from shares by the taxation law of one of the Contracting States and that is treated as a different class of income in the other State. They may also agree to the characterization of persons, the application of source rules to particular items of income, the meaning of a term, or the timing of an item of income.

The competent authorities also may agree as to the application of the provisions of domestic law regarding penalties, fines, and interest in a manner consistent with the purposes of the Convention.

Since the list under paragraph 3 is not exhaustive, the competent authorities may reach agreement on issues not enumerated in paragraph 3 if necessary to avoid double taxation. For example, the competent authorities may seek agreement on a uniform set of standards for the use of exchange rates. Agreements reached by the competent authorities under paragraph 3 need not conform to the internal law provisions of either Contracting State.

Finally, paragraph 3 authorizes the competent authorities to consult for the purpose of eliminating double taxation in cases not provided for in the Convention and to resolve any difficulties or doubts arising as to the interpretation or application of the Convention. This provision is intended to permit the competent authorities to implement the treaty in particular cases in a manner that is consistent with its expressed general purposes. It permits the competent authorities to deal with cases that are within the spirit of the provisions but that are not specifically covered. An example of such a case might be double taxation arising from a transfer pricing adjustment between two permanent establishments of a third-country resident, one in the United States and one in Iceland. Since no resident of a Contracting State is involved in the case, the Convention does not apply, but the competent authorities nevertheless may use the authority of this Article to prevent the double taxation of income.

Paragraph 4

Paragraph 4 provides that the competent authorities may communicate with each other for the purpose of reaching an agreement. This makes clear that the competent authorities of the two Contracting States may communicate without going through diplomatic channels. Such communication may be in various forms, including, where appropriate, through face-to-face meetings of representatives of the competent authorities.

Treaty termination in relation to competent authority dispute resolution

A case may be raised by a taxpayer after the Convention has been terminated with respect to a year for which a treaty was in force. In such a case the ability of the competent authorities to act is limited. They may not exchange confidential information, nor may they reach a solution that varies from that specified in its law.

Triangular competent authority solutions

International tax cases may involve more than two taxing jurisdictions (e.g., transactions among a parent corporation resident in country A and its subsidiaries resident in countries B and C). As long as there is a complete network of treaties among the three countries, it should be possible, under the full combination of bilateral authorities, for the competent authorities of the three States to work together on a three-sided solution. Although country A may not be able to give information received under Article 26 (Exchange of Information and Administrative Assistance) from country B to the authorities of country C, if the competent authorities of the three countries are working together, it should not be a problem for them to arrange for the authorities of country B to give the necessary information directly to the tax authorities of country C, as well as to those of country A. Each bilateral part of the trilateral solution must, of course, not exceed the scope of the authority of the competent authorities under the relevant bilateral treaty.

Relationship to Other Articles

This Article is not subject to the saving clause of paragraph 4 of Article 1 (General Scope) by virtue of the exceptions in subparagraph 5(a) of that Article. Thus, rules, definitions, procedures, etc. that are agreed upon by the competent authorities under this Article may be applied by the United States with respect to its citizens and residents even if they differ from the comparable Code provisions. Similarly, as indicated above, U.S. law may be overridden to provide refunds of tax to a U.S. citizen or resident under this Article. A person may seek relief under Article 24 regardless of whether he is generally entitled to benefits under Article 21 (Limitation on Benefits). As in all other cases, the competent authority is vested with the discretion to decide whether the claim for relief is justified.

ARTICLE 25 (EXCHANGE OF INFORMATION AND ADMINISTRATIVE ASSISTANCE)

This Article provides for the exchange of information and administrative assistance between the competent authorities of the Contracting States.

Paragraph 1

The obligation to obtain and provide information to the other Contracting State is set out in paragraph 1. The information to be exchanged is that which is relevant for carrying out the provisions of the Convention or the domestic laws of the United States or of the Iceland concerning taxes of every kind applied at the national level. Exchange of information with respect to each State's domestic law is authorized to the extent that taxation under domestic law is not contrary to the Convention. Thus, for example, information may be exchanged with respect to a covered tax, even if the transaction to which the information relates is a purely domestic transaction in the requesting State and, therefore, the exchange is not made to carry out the Convention. An example of such a case is provided in the OECD Commentary: a company resident in the United States and a company resident in Iceland transact business between themselves through a third-country resident company. Neither Contracting State has a treaty with the third State. To enforce their internal laws with respect to transactions of their residents with the third-country company (since there is no relevant treaty in force), the Contracting States may exchange information regarding the prices that their residents paid in their transactions with the third-country resident.

Paragraph 1 clarifies that information may be exchanged that relates to the assessment or collection of, the enforcement or prosecution in respect of, or the determination of appeals in relation to, the taxes covered by the Convention. Thus, the competent authorities may request and provide information for cases under examination or criminal investigation, in collection, on appeals, or under prosecution.

The taxes covered by the Convention for purposes of this Article constitute a broader category of taxes than those referred to in Article 2 (Taxes Covered). Exchange of information is authorized with respect to taxes of every kind imposed by a Contracting State at the national level. Accordingly, information may be exchanged with respect to U.S. estate and gift taxes, excise taxes or, with respect to Iceland, value added taxes.

Information exchange is not restricted by paragraph 1 of Article 1 (General Scope). Accordingly, information may be requested and provided under this article with respect to persons who are not residents of either Contracting State. For example, if a third-country resident has a permanent establishment in Iceland, and that permanent establishment engages in transactions with a U.S. enterprise, the United States could request information with respect to that permanent establishment, even though the third-country resident is not a resident of either Contracting State. Similarly, if a third-country resident maintains a bank account in Iceland, and the Internal Revenue Service has reason to believe that funds in that account should have been reported for U.S. tax purposes but have not been so reported, information can be requested from Iceland with respect to that person's account, even though that person is not the taxpayer under examination.

Although the term "United States" does not encompass U.S. possessions for most purposes of the Convention, Section 7651 of the Code authorizes the Internal Revenue Service to utilize the provisions of the Internal Revenue Code to obtain information from the U.S. possessions pursuant to a proper request made under Article 25. If necessary to obtain requested information, the Internal Revenue Service could issue and enforce an administrative summons to the taxpayer, a tax authority (or a government agency in a U.S. possession), or a third party located in a U.S. possession.

Paragraph 1 also provides assurances that any information exchanged will be treated as secret, subject to the same disclosure constraints as information obtained under the laws of the requesting State. Information received may be disclosed only to persons, including courts and administrative bodies, involved in the assessment, collection, or administration of, the enforcement or prosecution in respect of, or the determination of the of appeals in relation to, the taxes covered by the Convention. The information must be used by these persons in connection with the specified functions. Information may also be disclosed to legislative bodies, such as the tax-writing committees of Congress and the Government Accountability Office, engaged in the oversight of the preceding activities. Information received by these bodies must be for use in the performance of their role in overseeing the administration of U.S. tax laws. Information received may be disclosed in public court proceedings or in judicial decisions.

Paragraph 2

Paragraph 2 provides that when information is requested by a Contracting State in accordance with this Article, the other Contracting State is obligated to obtain the requested information as if the tax in question were the tax of the requested State, even if that State has no direct tax interest in the case to which the request relates. In the absence of such a paragraph, some taxpayers have argued that subparagraph 3(a) prevents a Contracting State from requesting information from a bank or fiduciary that the Contracting State does not need for its own tax purposes. This paragraph clarifies that paragraph 3 does not impose such a restriction and that a Contracting State is not limited to providing only the information that it already has in its own files.

Paragraph 3

Paragraph 3 provides that the obligations undertaken in paragraphs 1 and 2 to exchange information do not require a Contracting State to carry out administrative measures that are at variance with the laws or administrative practice of either State. Nor is a Contracting State required to supply information not obtainable under the laws or administrative practice of either State, or to disclose trade secrets or other information, the disclosure of which would be contrary to public policy.

Thus, a requesting State may be denied information from the other State if the information would be obtained pursuant to procedures or measures that are broader than those available in the requesting State. However, the statute of limitations of the Contracting State making the request for information should govern a request for information. Thus, the Contracting State of which the request is made should attempt to obtain the information even if its own statute of limitations has passed. In many cases, relevant information will still exist in the business records of the taxpayer or a third party, even though it is no longer required to be kept for domestic tax purposes.

While paragraph 3 states conditions under which a Contracting State is not obligated to comply with a request from the other Contracting State for information, the requested State is not precluded from providing such information, and may, at its discretion, do so subject to the limitations of its internal law.

Paragraph 7 of the Protocol provides that the powers of each Contracting State's competent authority to obtain information include powers to obtain information held by financial institutions, nominees, or persons acting in an agency or fiduciary capacity (not including information that would reveal confidential communications between a client and an attorney, solicitor, or other legal representative, where the client seeks legal advice), and information relating to the ownership of legal persons. Paragraph 7 of the Protocol acknowledges that each Contracting State's competent authority is able to exchange such information in accordance with Article 25. The provisions of paragraph 7 of the Protocol prevent a Contracting State from relying on paragraph 3 of the Convention to argue that its domestic bank secrecy laws (or similar legislation relating to disclosure of financial information by financial institutions or intermediaries) override its obligation to provide information under paragraph 1.

Paragraph 4

Paragraph 4 provides that the requesting State may specify the form in which information is to be provided (e.g., depositions of witnesses and authenticated copies of original documents).

The intention is to ensure that the information may be introduced as evidence in the judicial proceedings of the requesting State. The requested State should, if possible, provide the information in the form requested to the same extent that it can obtain information in that form under its own laws and administrative practices with respect to its own taxes.

Paragraph 5

Paragraph 5 provides for assistance in collection of taxes to the extent necessary to ensure that treaty benefits are enjoyed only by persons entitled to those benefits under the terms of the Convention. Under paragraph 5, a Contracting State will endeavor to collect on behalf of the other State only those amounts necessary to ensure that any exemption or reduced rate of tax at source granted under the Convention by that other State is not enjoyed by persons not entitled to those benefits. For example, if the payer of a U.S.-source portfolio dividend receives a Form W-8BEN or other appropriate documentation from the payee, the withholding agent is permitted to withhold at the portfolio dividend rate of 15 percent. If, however, the addressee is merely acting as a nominee on behalf of a third-country resident, paragraph 5 would obligate the other Iceland to withhold and remit to the United States the additional tax that should have been collected by the U.S. withholding agent.

This paragraph also makes clear that the Contracting State asked to collect the tax is not obligated, in the process of providing collection assistance, to carry out administrative measures that are different from those used in the collection of its own taxes, or that would be contrary to its sovereignty, security or public policy.

Paragraph 6

Paragraph 6 provides that a Contracting State must notify the competent authority of the other Contracting State before sending representatives to enter the requested State to interview individuals and examine books and records with the consent of the persons subject to examination.

ARTICLE 26 (MEMBERS OF DIPLOMATIC MISSIONS AND CONSULAR POSTS)

This Article confirms that any fiscal privileges to which diplomatic or consular officials are entitled under general provisions of international law or under special agreements will apply notwithstanding any provisions to the contrary in the Convention. The agreements referred to include any bilateral agreements, such as consular conventions, that affect the taxation of diplomats and consular officials and any multilateral agreements dealing with these issues, such as the Vienna Convention on Diplomatic Relations and the Vienna Convention on Consular Relations. The U.S. generally adheres to the latter because its terms are consistent with customary international law.

The Article does not independently provide any benefits to diplomatic agents and consular officers. Article 18 (Government Service) does so, as do Code section 893 and a number of bilateral and multilateral agreements. In the event that there is a conflict between the Convention and international law or such other treaties, under which the diplomatic agent or consular official is entitled to greater benefits under the latter, the latter laws or agreements shall have precedence. Conversely, if the Convention confers a greater benefit than another agreement, the affected person could claim the benefit of the tax treaty.

Pursuant to subparagraph 5(b) of Article 1 (General Scope), the saving clause of paragraph 4 of Article 1 does not apply to override any benefits of this Article available to an individual who is neither a citizen of the United States nor has immigrant status in the United States.

ARTICLE 27 (ENTRY INTO FORCE)

This Article contains the rules for bringing the Convention into force and giving effect to its provisions.

Paragraph 1

Paragraph 1 provides that the Convention is subject to ratification in accordance with the applicable procedures of the United States and Iceland. Further, the Contracting States shall notify each other by written notification, through diplomatic channels, when their respective applicable procedures have been satisfied.

In the United States, the process leading to ratification and entry into force is as follows: Once a treaty has been signed by authorized representatives of the two Contracting States, the Department of State sends the treaty to the President who formally transmits it to the Senate for its advice and consent to ratification, which requires approval by two-thirds of the Senators present and voting. Prior to this vote, however, it generally has been the practice for the Senate Committee on Foreign Relations to hold hearings on the treaty and make a recommendation regarding its approval to the full Senate. Both Government and private sector witnesses may testify at these hearings. After the Senate gives its advice and consent to ratification of the treaty, an instrument of ratification is drafted for the President's signature. The President's signature completes the process in the United States.

Paragraph 2

Paragraph 2 provides that the Convention will enter into force on the date of the later of the notifications referred to in paragraph 1. The relevant date is the date on the second of these notification documents, and not the date on which the second notification is provided to the other Contracting State. The date on which a treaty enters into force is not necessarily the date on which its provisions take effect. Paragraph 2, therefore, also contains rules that determine when the provisions of the treaty will have effect.

Under subparagraph 2(a), the Convention will have effect with respect to taxes withheld at source (principally dividends, interest and royalties) for income derived on or after the first day of January in the first calendar year following the date on which the Convention enters into force. For all other taxes, subparagraph 2(b) specifies that the Convention will have effect for taxes chargeable for any tax year beginning on or after January 1 of the year following entry into force.

Paragraph 3

Paragraph 3 provides an exception to the general rule of paragraph 2. Under paragraph 3, if the prior income tax convention between the United States and Iceland would have afforded greater relief from tax than this Convention, that prior convention shall, at the election of any person that was entitled to benefits under the prior convention, continue to have effect in its entirety for a twelve-month period from the date on which this Convention otherwise would have had effect with respect to such person.

Thus, a taxpayer may elect to extend the benefits of the prior convention for one year from the date on which the relevant provision of the new Convention would first take effect. During the period in which the election is in effect, the provisions of the prior convention will continue to apply only insofar as they applied before the entry into force of the Convention. If the grace period is elected, all of the provisions of the prior convention must be applied for that additional year. The taxpayer may not apply certain, more favorable provisions of the prior convention and, at the same time, apply other, more favorable provisions of this Convention. The taxpayer must choose one convention in its entirety or the other.

The prior convention shall terminate on the last date on which it has effect with respect to any tax in accordance with the provisions of Article 28.

Paragraph 4

Paragraph 4 provides that an individual who was entitled to benefits under Article 21 (Teachers) of the prior convention at the time of the entry into force of this Convention is "grandfathered," and will continue to be entitled to the benefits available under the prior convention until such time as that individual would cease to be entitled to benefits if the prior convention remained in force.

ARTICLE 28 (TERMINATION)

The Convention is to remain in effect indefinitely, unless terminated by one of the Contracting States in accordance with the provisions of Article 28. The Convention may be terminated by giving notice of termination in writing at least six months before the end of any calendar year. If notice of termination is given, the provisions of the Convention with respect to withholding at source will cease to have effect on income derived on or after the first day of January in the first calendar year following the year in which notice is given. For other taxes, the Convention will cease to have effect for taxes chargeable for any tax year beginning on or after the first day of January in the first calendar year following the year in which notice is given.

Article 28 relates only to unilateral termination of the Convention by a Contracting State. Nothing in that Article should be construed as preventing the Contracting States from concluding a new bilateral agreement, subject to ratification, that supersedes, amends or terminates provisions of the Convention without the notification period.

Customary international law observed by the United States and other countries, as reflected in the Vienna Convention on Treaties, allows termination by one Contracting State at any time in the event of a "material breach" of the agreement by the other Contracting State.

www.ingramcontent.com/pod-product-compliance
Lightning Source LLC
Chambersburg PA
CBHW060443110626
46523CB00042B/611